The Doctrine of Prayer

T. W. Hunt

Convention Press
Nashville, Tennessee

Unless stated otherwise, the Scripture quotations
in this book are from the *New American Standard Bible*.
Copyright © The Lockman Foundation,
1960, 1962, 1963, 1968, 1971, 1972, 1973, 1975, 1977.
Used by permission.

5133-12

This book is the text for course 05052
in the subject area Baptist Doctrine
in the Church Study Course

Dewey Decimal Classification Number: 248.3
Subject Heading: PRAYER

Printed in the United States of America

Church Training Department
The Sunday School Board of the Southern Baptist Convention
127 Ninth Avenue, North
Nashville, Tennessee 37234

Contents

About the Authors

T. W. Hunt was born in Mammoth Spring, Arkansas. He did his undergraduate work at Ouachita University and holds a master's degree and a PhD from North Texas State University.

Dr. Hunt's professional background includes teaching at the public school and college levels. Since 1963 he has been professor of church music at Southwestern Baptist Theological Seminary, Fort Worth, Texas.

Dr. Hunt conducts seminars on prayer for churches and denominational assemblies across the United States.

The teaching guide for this book was written by Arthur H. Criscoe. Dr. Criscoe is the director of the Management Support Group, Church Training Department of The Sunday School Board of the Southern Baptist Convention. He is also the author of *The Doctrine of Prayer—Teaching Workbook*.

Preface

So many writers, preachers, and teachers have influenced my prayer life and my understanding of prayer that it would be impossible to list them or credit them properly. Prayer is an ancient subject and has gripped the attention of minds and spirits far greater than mine throughout history. But there is one credit I cannot ignore. Years ago I met a man of prayer, of such great faith that I remained constantly astonished as I got to know him. His name was Bob Maulden.

Bob kept a prayer room in his home and in his business, a Christian book store. I quickly learned that he was available for prayer at any hour of the day or night. Sometimes I would call him with a prayer request, and he would turn a sale over to a clerk in order to go immediately to prayer. He was at his church every Sunday morning at 6:00 AM and would pray until other people began to arrive. His widow, Bea, also a prayer warrior to whom I am greatly indebted, told me that many times he prayed all night. I had never known anyone so completely given to prayer. Bob's faith so intrigued me that I began studying the prayers of the Bible, and my own prayer life was transformed. Bob went to be with the Lord in February of 1982, but his legacy lives on in the lives of many who were changed by the power of his prayers. I am one of those, and this book is gratefully dedicated to him.

Another prayerful couple in Fort Worth made this book possible by the gift of the computer and word processor on which this book was written. It would have been impossible without their gift and their prayers, but they prefer to remain anonymous. Still, I must acknowledge a profound debt to their enabling.

My wife and my daughter patiently read the manuscript, made helpful suggestions, and, most importantly, supported me with the best support anyone can give—prayer. And every day of my life I have been prayed for by the two persons who were God's instrument to give me physical life and to lead me into eternal life—my parents. This book owes much to my family.

My supreme debt is to the Father of Light who gives light. Even the people who have blessed me were His gift to me. He is the source of my knowledge and of the insights of my teachers. My prayer is that when God's people read this book, they will see the validity of His method and will grant Him the pleasure He has asked throughout time—the pleasure of their company.

Chapter 1

The Foundation

# of Prayer—the God Who Cares

Prayer Is Universal
Prayer Is Based on the Nature of God
Prayer Is Effective Because God Has Chosen to Hear
  When We Call to Him

Prayer must be built on the foundation of the sovereignty and character of God. Prayer is as old as man, permeates all of history, and is common to all people. Scripturally, prayer is universal in time, in space, and in the scope of its content.

We read in the Bible about men praying (Hezekiah, Paul), women praying (Miriam, Anna), and children praying (Samuel, Josiah). Humans are unique among God's creatures; made in the likeness of God, they alone are in a condition to have fellowship with God.

Prayer Is Universal
Genesis pictures God as introducing Adam to His world. Evidently the Lord and Adam walked together, talked together, and enjoyed a sharing which is characteristic of beings with common interests. There can be no doubt that Adam enjoyed an unspoiled fellowship with God prior to his fall. That sort of dialogue can perhaps be called a type of prayer. Surely Abel also, who knew how to offer a sacrifice pleasing to God, must have addressed some sort of prayer to God. After Abel's murder, God gave Eve a son, Seth, whose name means "appointed"; that is, he was appointed in the place of Abel (Gen. 4:25). It was through this line (not Cain's line, but through the replacement for righteous Abel) that a significant new dimension of fellowship with

God was introduced into human history.

To Seth was born Enosh, whose name means "man," or even "weakness" or "mortality." *Adam* means "man," generically as human, but now he is Enosh, man in his weakness. As the slowly developing awareness of the dreadful separation sin had imposed permeated the consciousness of this new generation, a sense of yearning and need moved man to reach out to the only source that could meet that need. To Enosh, to one who was frail and realized his dependence on God, was granted the privilege of marking an important milestone in prayer history: "To Seth, to him also a son was born; and he called his name Enosh. Then men began to call upon the name of the Lord" (Gen. 4:26).

This calling upon the name of the Lord would characterize God's people from the time of Enosh onward. Abraham *called* upon the name of the Lord (Gen. 12:8); in Elijah's great contest with Baal, he *called* upon Jehovah (1 Kings 18:24). The same idea becomes a part of a divine promise in Psalm 145:18: "The Lord is near to all who call upon Him, to all who call upon Him in truth." Isaiah urges us to "Seek the Lord while He may be found; call upon Him while He is near" (55:6). Indignation threatens those who do not call upon the Lord: "Pour out Thy wrath upon the nations which do not know Thee, and upon the kingdoms which do not call upon Thy name" (Ps. 79:6). The practice continued throughout the entire biblical period. In the New Testament that calling out to God became a calling out to Christ; Paul addressed his first Corinthian letter to "all who in every place call upon the name of our Lord Jesus Christ" (1:2). Peter's sermon at Pentecost, quoting Joel's prophecy of universal opportunity for salvation (Joel 2:32), promises that whoever calls on the name of the Lord will be saved (Acts 2:21).

Prayer, then, is universal throughout *time*. Men called on

the Lord as soon as they realized that in their frailty they needed Him. This was from the dawn of history. The greatest men and women—Moses, Abraham, Hannah, Mary—were people of prayer. From Genesis to Malachi, from Matthew to Revelation, the record shows that the lives of biblical saints were characterized by prayer. The next-to-last verse in the Bible is a prayer (Rev. 22:20). Throughout the Bible and throughout the ages, prayer has sustained the people of God.

Prayer is also universal in *space*. It knows no geographical, racial, or ethnic lines. The word *all* is one of the most important words in the Bible. The psalmist sang, "O Thou who dost hear prayer, to Thee all men come" (Ps. 65:2). Jesus declared, " 'I, if I be lifted up from the earth, will draw all men to Myself' " (John 12:32). Therefore Paul could write in Romans 10:13, " 'Whoever will call upon the name of the Lord will be saved.' " In 1 Kings 8:41-43 Solomon prayed for the day when all people of the earth would know and fear Jehovah. Psalm 86:9 predicts a universal worship of the one true God: "All nations whom Thou hast made shall come and worship before Thee, O Lord, and they shall glorify Thy name."

Prayer pervades the two great dimensions of time and space because God Himself is universal. He is in all dimensions, in all times, and in all places. He expects to meet people wherever they find themselves. The various manners of meeting with God become various kinds of prayer. The only conditions God places on the meeting time or the meeting place are those which bound and demonstrate His own character.

Prayer Is Based on the Nature of God

Any address to a superior must be based on the character and position of that person. Jesus taught us to begin our prayers with an affirmation of the holiness of God's name

(Matt. 6:9). In most of the divine encounters in the Bible, the first attribute of God recognized by those who met Him was holiness. When Moses saw the burning bush on Mount Horeb, he heard a voice say, "'Do not come near here; remove your sandals from your feet, for the place on which you are standing is holy ground'" (Ex. 3:5). When Isaiah saw the vision of God in the Temple, the seraphim cried out, "'Holy, Holy, Holy, is the Lord of hosts'" (Isa. 6:3). Daniel knew he could not pray apart from God's righteousness; in the famous prayer after his terrifying visions he acknowledged, "'Righteousness belongs to Thee, O Lord'" (Dan. 9:7). When Peter recognized the awesome identity of Jesus, he fell at Jesus' feet and cried out, "'Depart from me, for I am a sinful man, O Lord!'" (Luke 5:8).

But the seemingly opposite side of God's character is His mercy toward sinners. James describes Him as being compassionate and merciful (5:11). Many of the psalms (86:15; 145:8) sing lyrically of this attracting aspect of God's nature; Psalm 103:8-12 describes the extent to which God will forgive sins:

The Lord is compassionate and gracious, slow to anger and abounding in lovingkindness. He will not always strive with us; nor will He keep His anger forever. He has not dealt with us according to our sins, nor rewarded us according to our iniquities. For as high as the heavens are above the earth, so great is His lovingkindness toward those who fear Him. As far as the east is from the west, so far has He removed our transgressions from us.

God's awesome holiness seems to separate Him from sinful people, but His tenderness for His creatures draws Him close to us. It seems illogical that a God so terrifyingly holy also could be so "plenteous in mercy" (Ps. 103:8, KJV).

The implication is that the Lord is *wealthy* in mercy! It is unmistakably certain in the Bible that God is infinitely holy and at the same time compassionate toward sinful people. This paradox, like many other Bible paradoxes, gives us God's way of "enclosing infinity" for finite minds. Although we can never fully understand this paradox, it contains the truth about the nature of God.

Prayer can have no meaning unless it takes into account God's total nature. He is holy; we come to Him on those grounds. He is love; we pray knowing that He is concerned about our needs. Because He is merciful, God understands and cares about human need. In most of the prayers of biblical characters, God took the initiative. It is that initiating God who tells us: "'Ask, and it shall be given to you; seek, and you shall find; knock, and it shall be opened to you. For everyone who asks receives, and he who seeks finds, and to him who knocks it shall be opened'" (Matt. 7:7-8). The greatest saints have always known intuitively, from the depths of their spiritual nature, that God desires to provide for His own. Abraham assured Isaac as he was preparing to ascend Mount Moriah, "'God will provide for Himself the lamb for the burnt offering'" (Gen. 22:8). Only one who grasped the truth that God is concerned about human need could cry out, "The Lord is my shepherd" (Ps. 23:1) or "The Lord is your keeper" (Ps. 121:5). Supremely, it is Jesus who assures us with the most graphic pictures that God is deeply concerned for our needs. He asked, as though it were the most reasonable question imaginable, "'If God so arrays the grass of the field, which is alive today and tomorrow is thrown into the furnace, will He not much more do so for you, O men of little faith?'" (Matt. 6:30).

God has chosen to relate Himself to us as a loving Father. Jesus told us to address Him as "our Father" (Matt. 6:9). Only a divine Father would want to number our hairs (Matt. 10:30)! Jesus asks a question in Matthew 7:11 that is really a logical affirmation: "'If you then, being evil, know how to give good gifts to your children, how much more shall your Father who is in heaven give what is good to those who ask Him!'"

And it is not only as Father that God demonstrates His infinite concern. The Bible provides us with other characterizations of God that bring Him close. He is also shepherd, keeper, refuge and strength, a very present help in trouble (Ps. 46:1), and a sun and shield (Ps. 84:11). Christ established the nearness of God in even more intimate terms. If He is brother (Heb. 2:11), we are His brothers and sisters. If He is bridegroom (Mark 2:19), we are His bride. If He is teacher (John 3:2), we are His disciples. If He is the vine, we are His own branches (John 15:5). He almost exhausts language to clarify for us how caring He is and how intimate with us He wants to be.

PERSONAL LEARNING ACTIVITY 1

Can you recall a time in your life when you were especially aware of God's caring for you? Use the space below to write about that experience.

Prayer Is Effective Because God Has Chosen to Hear When We Call to Him

God obviously hears all things, and yet He says He "hears" the prayers of His children in a special way. How can one say to an all-hearing God, "'Thou art my God; give ear, O

Lord, to the voice of my supplications'" (Ps. 140:6)? Sometimes the word *hear* in Hebrew carries the idea of "respond to," as in Zechariah 10:6: "'For I am the Lord their God, and I will answer [the King James Version says *hear*] them.'" The certainty of His hearing is established by Psalm 116:1-2: "I love the Lord, because He hears my voice and my supplications. Because He has inclined His ear to me, therefore I shall call upon Him as long as I live." The word for *hear* in Psalm 116:1 is the same as that in Zechariah 10:6—God *hears, answers,* or *responds to.*

God is personal, and He relates to human need in a personal way. Again and again, we find *persons* appealing to God as a *Person.* Exodus 33:13-14 gives us a remarkably personal dialogue between Moses and God. Moses pleaded, "'Now therefore, I pray Thee, if I have found favor in Thy sight, let me know Thy ways, that I may know Thee, so that I may find favor in Thy sight.'" God answered, "'My presence shall go with you, and I will give you rest.'" David's plea for forgiveness in Psalm 51 would have no meaning if it did not become poignantly personal: "Do not cast me away from Thy presence, and do not take Thy Holy Spirit from me" (v. 11). The joy of God's personal presence is described rapturously in Psalm 16:11: "In Thy presence is fulness of joy; in Thy right hand there are pleasures forever."

Fellowship is a mark of personhood. God is actively seeking fellowship with persons whose hearts are like His. Hanani the seer told King Asa that "'the eyes of the Lord move to and fro throughout the earth that He may strongly support those whose heart is completely His'" (2 Chron. 16:9). Peter makes Psalm 34:15 a part of the New Testament message: "For the eyes of the Lord are upon the righteous, and His ears attend to their prayer'" (1 Pet. 3:12).

Friendship is a mark of personhood. What do people do in personal fellowship? They talk, walk, and share. Bible history is replete with individuals who enjoyed an intimate relationship with God. We are told that Enoch "walked with God three hundred years" (Gen. 5:22) and also that Noah "walked with God" (Gen. 6:9). In Isaiah 41:8 God calls Abraham His friend. James 2:23 makes it clear that Abraham's faith, not his performance, earned him this title: "The Scripture was fulfilled which says, 'And Abraham believed God, and it was reckoned to him as righteousness,' and he was called the friend of God."

The prayer of an individual is heard by God. The psalmist expressed gratitude for answers in the past. He wrote, "In my distress I called upon the Lord, and cried to my God for help; He heard my voice out of His temple, and my cry for help before Him came into His ears" (Ps. 18:6). He also expressed confidence in future answers. He wrote, "My voice rises to God, and I will cry aloud; my voice rises to God, and He will hear me" (Ps. 77:1). The Christian is assured that through Christ we "have our access in one Spirit to the Father" (Eph. 2:18).

The Old Testament preserves beautiful instances of answers to the prayers of individuals. Two examples are Hannah's prayer for a son (1 Sam. 1:10-17,19) and Hezekiah's prayer to live (2 Kings 20:1-5). The New Testament furnishes us with moving examples in the early church, such as Peter's prayer for Tabitha in Acts 9:40. Numerous petitions for healing are directed to Christ in the Gospels. Such prayers also appear in the writings of Paul.

History, then, demonstrates that God is sovereign and yet desires the fellowship of those He has created. Prayer grows out of God's own nature and His plans for us. His plans involve all people, so all may come to Him, and He delights to hear them when they pray. Prayer is the shaping force of history. God used Moses' prayers to preserve Israel through the wandering years; He used Nehemiah's prayer to make possible the rebuilding of the wall around

Jerusalem; Jesus' prayers shaped His disciples and helped to develop them into the kind of people that would populate a new kind of kindgom; Paul's prayers were God's instrument for shaping the personality and destiny of the new church as it spread across the Mediterranean world. In the Bible, prayer is the amazing cooperation of mankind in bringing God's plans for this world to fruition. It is true that God could move unilaterally because He is sovereign. Yet, it is His wisdom that persons share with Him His own divine work. An important part of that divine work is done through prayer.

PERSONAL LEARNING ACTIVITY 2

The author of this book says, "Prayer is the shaping force of history." Do you agree or disagree with this statement? List some biblical examples of this statement. _Yes I do. Perhaps Simeon's prayer aided Christs decision. Daniels & three prayed for the interpretation of Neb's dream, therefore led him to praise the one true God. Abrahams prayer saved Lot. (He should have prayed for Lots wife also. Solomon effectively governed Israel because he prayed for wisdom_

Chapter 2

Jesus—

the Example of Prayer

The Prayer Life of Jesus
Jesus Taught His Followers to Pray
Prayer in the Believer's Life

Jesus was a man of prayer. The earliest utterance recorded from the lips of Jesus (Luke 2:49) occurred in what He later called a "house of prayer." Isaiah had so named it (Isa. 56:7), and it is probable that *that* function—prayer—was important in Jesus' own view of the Temple. It was His Father's house (John 2:16), and the outrage of the money changers was that an activity so foreign to the spirit of prayer should find a place in the Temple.

The writer of Hebrews pictured the prayers of Jesus vividly: "In the days of His flesh, He offered up both prayers and supplications with loud crying and tears to the One able to save Him from death, and He was heard because of His piety" (Heb. 5:7). The translators of the *New American Standard Bible* infer from the verb form in Luke 5:16 that Jesus' withdrawals for prayer were continual: "He Himself would *often* slip away to the wilderness and pray."

The Prayer Life of Jesus
The occasions for His prayers were many and varied. He prayed in the early morning (Mark 1:35) and at night (Matt. 14:23). He often prayed alone. This must have impressed John, who piled up phrases to intensify the solitariness of some of Jesus' prayers: He "withdrew again to the mountain by Himself alone" (John 6:15). Any of the three

and He prayed for us
Lk. 17.

expressions—"withdrew," "by Himself," and "alone"—
would have indicated seclusion, yet John felt compelled to
provide all three. He prayed with others present (Matt.
11:25-26), and He prayed in large public gatherings (Matt.
14:19). Luke tells us He prayed all night (Luke 6:12).

Sometimes He is pictured as praying during one of His
miracles (John 11:41-42). On four different occasions He is
described as blessing a meal (Luke 9:16; 24:30; Matt. 15:36;
26:26-27). Twice He blessed people. He blessed the children
who were brought to Him (Matt. 19:13-15). He also blessed
His disciples as He parted from them at the time of the
ascension (Luke 24:50).

Major decisions in His life were preceded by prayer. Since
"the Spirit impelled Him" (Mark 1:12) into the wilderness
for the temptation by Satan, it is likely that He was in a state
of prayer after His baptism. His decision to leave Capernaum and preach in "the other cities also" followed the
prayer in "a lonely place" of Mark 1:35 and Luke 4:42-43.
One of the most significant decisions of His life, the
choosing of the twelve apostles, came after a night of prayer
(Luke 6:12-13). Evidently there were a number of "disciples" from whom He could have chosen, for "He called His
disciples to Him; and chose twelve of them," so He must
have prayed about many people before He chose the
twelve. Mark indicates the weightiness of this decision in
the fact that these men were to have authority (Mark 3:15).

Supremely, the great personal crises of His life were
intense moments of prayer. It was in Gethsemane that He
fell on His face (Matt. 26:39) and addressed God with the
intimate title *Abba* (Mark 14:36). Mark and Luke simply
reported His agonizing request that the cup be taken from
Him, along with His commitment to the will of God.
Matthew recorded that the second and third prayers
specifically detailed His determination to carry out the will
of God: "'My Father, if this cannot pass away unless I drink

it, Thy will be done'" (Matt. 26:42). The final utterance of His life was also a commitment in prayer: "'Father, into Thy hands I commit My spirit'" (Luke 23:46). The importance of these prayers cannot be overstated. They were part of events that have significance for all of us.

PERSONAL LEARNING ACTIVITY 3

Read the following statements about the prayer life of Jesus. Which statements are true? Which are false? Circle your answer.

1. T F Jesus often prayed early in the morning.
2. T F There is no record of Jesus praying in public.
3. T F Jesus chose His disciples after praying all night.
4. T F When Jesus prayed in Gethsemane, He expressed unwillingness to die on the cross.
5. T F The final recorded words of Jesus before He died were words of prayer.

Answers: 1. T, 2. F, 3. T, 4. F, 5. T

The most sublime and noble prayer in the Bible is the high-priestly prayer of Christ in John 17. It speaks of the eternal redemptive work of Christ and His relationship to the Father. It also contains petitions to the Father that are important to all people. These various factors demonstrate an interworking that is remarkable in its unity. The opening five verses record Jesus' prayer for Himself; the rest of the prayer is on behalf of His disciples and those who would follow Him through the centuries.

His prayer for Himself may be summed up in verse 5: "'Now, glorify Thou Me together with Thyself, Father, with the glory which I had with Thee before the world was.'" Christ's prayer is for the restoration of the right order of things which had existed from all eternity. The work of redemption should properly be climaxed by His lordship over all creation and headship over the church. Rainsford sums it up:

> *He asks His Father to take the Son of Man into the position He as the Son of God occupied before His incarnation; that there, as the Representative of His people, and as Head of His Church, and Head over all things to His Church, He might rule everything in heaven, and earth, and hell, for their benefit. The prayer means nothing less than that; God only knows how much more it means.*[1]

The background of the Lord's petitions on behalf of His disciples parallels His sense of identity with the Father (vv. 6-12) to the identity of His disciples with Himself (vv. 12-22). These two facts follow the pattern of His prayer for Himself and His prayer for the disciples. This paralleling of relationships is important because it serves as background and basis for His requests on behalf of His disciples.

His first identity with the Father is at the point of the divine glory: "'Glorify Thy Son, that the Son may glorify Thee'" (v. 1); "glorify Thou Me together with Thyself'" (v. 5). From any other lips such a prayer would be blasphemy; from Christ, it is a self-identity with the deity of the Father. Jesus claimed the name of the Father: "'Keep them in Thy name, the name which Thou hast given Me'" (v. 11). His disciples were first those of His Father: "'Thine they were, and Thou gavest them to Me'" (v. 6). He identified with His Father in their common possessions: "'All things that are Mine are Thine, and Thine are Mine'" (v. 10). The work of the Father and the Son was also identical; after asking the Father to keep them in the Father's name, He said this keeping would be a continuation of His own work: "'While I was with them, I was keeping them in thy name'" (v. 12). Christ identified with the Father in a common glory, a common name, common disciples, common possessions, and a common work. He identified with the Father's deity and shared His glory.

His identity with the disciples was along the lines of their humanity. Their joy was the same as the joy of Jesus: "'These things I speak in the world, that they may have My joy made full in themselves'" (v. 13). His disciples were not of the world, even as He was not of the world (v. 16). The mission of Christ and His disciples was identical: "'As Thou didst send Me into the world, I also have sent them into the world'" (v. 18). He identified their sanctification with His: "'For their sakes I sanctify Myself, that they themselves also may be sanctified in truth'" (v. 19). He even shared His glory with the disciples: "'The glory which Thou hast given Me I have given to them'" (v. 22). Christ identified with His disciples in a common joy, a common separation, a common mission, a common sanctification, and a common glory. There is a progression in these lines from joy to glory.

Having established the reality of His relationship to His Father and His followers, Jesus interwove five specific petitions for the disciples.

- "'Holy Father, keep them in Thy name'" (v. 11), more specifically stated in verse 15, "Keep them from the evil one'";
- "'Sanctify them in the truth'" (v. 17);
- "'that they also may be in Us'" (v. 21);
- "'Father, I desire that they also, whom Thou hast given Me, be with Me where I am'" (v. 24); and
- "'that they may all be one'" (v. 21, repeated as concomitants of other facts in vv. 11, 22, and 23).

Other statements in the prayer are actually consequences of one of His statements or requests. If we are one in the Father and the Son, the world will believe that the Father sent the Son (v. 21). If we are perfected in unity, the world will know that the Father sent the Son and that the Father loved the disciples as He loved the Son (v. 23). The fact that Christ makes the Father's name known will cause the Father's love to be in the disciples (v. 26). These are not requests but are prayerful recognitions of the right order of things. They are important because they are the clearest specimen we have of Christ's prayer as High Priest.

This was not the only occasion on which Christ prayed for others; see, for example, His prayer for Peter in Luke 22:32. But it is extremely instructive. John 17 is the longest of Christ's recorded prayers. It exhibits a profound sense of self-identity, provides a divine basis for God the Father to answer the prayers, and, in view of its occasion (the night before He gave His life), demonstrates the most powerful faith of all the prayers of the Bible.

PERSONAL LEARNING ACTIVITY 4

Read the prayer of Jesus in John 17. Find as many petitions in that prayer that apply to Christians today as you can. List those petitions below. *Verse 6, 7 — 11*

14, 15, 16, 17, 18, 19, 20 - 26

Jesus Taught His Followers to Pray

Most of the writers of the New Testament included some teaching on prayer in their letters, but the most extensive statements of principles of prayer were those of Jesus. Jesus' most detailed statement of His training program for His disciples is the Sermon on the Mount. A significant portion of that program is devoted to His teaching on prayer.

He first told His disciples how *not* to pray (Matt. 6:5-8), and then He gave a model of the ideal directions prayer *should* take (Matt. 6:9-14). The negative teaching included two strong prohibitions. In each, the prayer of the disciple is compared to a false kind of prayer; the disciple is not to pray as the religious hypocrites, for display, and we are not to pray as pagans, babbling meaninglessly.

In the command to avoid display, Jesus demonstrated His high regard for the holy. His own example commended His emphasis on privacy. Later He would warn about the scribes who "'for appearance's sake offer long [public] prayers'" (Mark 12:40). Jesus' command to His disciples was, "When thou prayest, thou shalt not be as the hypocrites" (Matt. 6:5, KJV). His emphasis on privacy is underlined by the singular pronoun. He further emphasized the importance of privacy by stating the command in a positive form: the individual is to go into an inner room, shut out the world, and pray to the Father who is in secret (see Matt. 6:6).

The second negative command, like all the rest of Jesus' teaching on prayer, is given in the plural and has general application: we are not to use "meaningless repetition," or to babble endlessly. This does not prohibit long prayers, for Jesus prayed all night (Luke 6:12). Every recorded example of lengthy prayer by Jesus was in private. The command to avoid babbling is a reminder that God does not need information and prefers that our prayers be to the point. The disciples would have been aware of the hours-long wail of the priests of Baal in their contest with Elijah on Mount Carmel. They "called on the name of Baal from morning until noon saying, 'O Baal, answer us'" (1 Kings 18:26). This was in sharp contrast to the brief, to-the-point prayer of Elijah to the Lord (see 1 Kings 18:36-37).

Jesus repeatedly emphasized the importance of faith in our prayers. At the foot of the Mount of Transfiguration, when the disciples failed to cast out a demon, He told them, "'If you have faith as a mustard seed, you shall say to this mountain, "Move from here to there," and it shall move; and nothing shall be impossible to you'" (Matt. 17:20). He repeated this illustration after the disciples were amazed over the withering of a fig tree He had cursed: "'Truly I say to you, if you have faith, and do not doubt, you shall not only do what was done to the fig tree, but even if you say to this mountain, "Be taken up and cast into the sea," it shall happen. And all things you ask in prayer, believing, you shall receive'" (Matt. 21:21-22).

The Model Prayer, or the disciples' prayer, teaches us to address God as our Father. In His teaching on prayer, Jesus repeatedly referred to God as "'your Father'" (Matt. 6:6,15). In the Synoptic Gospels, He is often "'your heavenly Father'" (Matt. 6:14; Luke 11:13) or "'your Father who is in heaven'" (Matt. 7:11; Mark 11:25,26). In John, He is usually "'the Father'" (John 14:13; 15:16; 16:23,26,27). Jesus introduced us to a relationship with God in an intimacy that had not been emphasized up to His time.

In the Model Prayer, content is important and order is important. There are six petitions, divided in two equal parts. The first three are concerned with God's nature and purposes. We are to pray on behalf of the holiness of God's name, the primacy of His sovereignty, and the accomplishment of His purposes on earth:

Hallowed be Thy name.
Thy kingdom come.
Thy will be done, on earth as it is in heaven.

The second group of petitions is on behalf of the petitioners. One petition has to do with the supplying of (physical needs.) The other two are for the supplying of spiritual needs—for sustenance, the restoration of fellowship with God through forgiveness, and the maintenance of fellowship through protection from temptation.

> *Give us this day our daily bread.*
> *And forgive us our debts, as we also have forgiven*
>   *our debtors.*
> *And do not lead us into temptation, but deliver us*
>   *from evil.*

In the prayer for forgiveness, Christ made it plain that forgiveness is possible for us because our willingness to forgive identifies us with God in His forgiving character. Later, in Gethsemane, he would amplify and emphasize the prayer for deliverance from temptation by admonishing the disciples to "'keep watching and praying, that you may not enter into temptation'" (Matt. 26:41). In the latter passage, Christ made it clear that even a willing spirit can succumb to the weakness of the flesh. The only way to overcome the flesh is to be constantly vigilant in prayer.

Jesus assured His followers of the goodness of God to hear and answer prayer. He told us that the human actions of asking, seeking, and knocking would be met with such divine response that we in turn will receive, will find, and will face an open door (Matt. 7:7-8). God's nature is such that asking elicits His giving, seeking obtains His guidance, and knocking reveals a divinely opened opportunity. Many times in His teaching on prayer, Jesus used the word *ask*. He assured us that our Heavenly Father knows better how to give good gifts than human parents (Matt. 7:9-11). He said the Father is more disposed to supply need than a friend (Luke 11:5-13). He said also that God is more ready to dispense justice than an earthly judge (Luke 18:1-8). In each of these illustrations, Jesus pictured God as going far beyond any human measure. If an earthly father will give good gifts to his child, how *much more* will the Heavenly Father do so (Matt. 7:11)? If a friend will supply need, how *much more* will the Heavenly Father give the Holy Spirit (Luke 11:13)? If an unjust judge will administer protection, will God delay long in providing for His elect (Luke 18:7)?

What is it that God will give? The answer of Jesus is: "'what you need'" (Matt. 6:8); "'good gifts'" and "'what is good'" (Matt. 7:11); "'anything that [two agreed] they may ask'" (Matt. 18:19); "'all things you ask in prayer, believing'" (Matt. 21:22); "'legal protection'" and "'justice for His elect'" (Luke 18:5,7); "'whatever you ask in My name'" (John 14:13); and, most comprehensive of all, "'anything'" (John 16:23). He sets no limits on what God is willing to give and describes it all as "good."

Prayer in the Believer's Life

Jesus taught the importance of prayer in the believer's life. Two of His most powerful parables encourage His disciples to pray persistently. In Luke 11:5-13 He pictured one who should have been favorably disposed, a friend, who yielded to an insistent demand for an emergency food supply. In Luke 18:1-8 He told of one *un*favorably disposed, an unjust judge, who yielded to a widow's stubborn suit for protection.

In both parables, Jesus was stressing the importance of persistence; He centered on the character of the supplicant rather than the one addressed. Persistence indicated something in their character which was pleasing to God. In the first story Jesus concluded, "'I tell you, even though he will not get up and give him anything because he is his friend, yet because of his persistence he will get up and give him as much as he needs'" (Luke 11:8). Persistence secured as much or more than the original request for three loaves. The clear implication is that God is even more willing than a friend to respond to our needs (see vv. 9-10). In the second story the same idea of God's willingness to go beyond our expectations is evident. After demonstrating the willingness of the judge to yield to persistence, the Lord gave one of the most thrilling pictures in Scripture of God's readiness to hear: " 'Hear what the unrighteous judge said; now shall not God bring about justice for His elect, who cry to Him day and night, and will He delay long over them? I tell you that He will bring about justice for them speedily' " (Luke 18:6-8). This parable is a study in contrast. God is not at all like the unrighteous judge. He is eager to hear the cries of His people.

It may seem strange that God should require importunity. Biblical examples of importunity furnish us with many object lessons of its value. Persistence gives time to be sure of what we want and of what God prefers to give in His desire for our good. In Abraham's reiterated requests for the sparing of Sodom and Gomorrah, he began with a dwarfed conception of God; he feared that God would destroy a community of fifty righteous pocketed in sinful cities. He ended with a magnificent understanding of God's holiness and mercy; God would have spared Sodom even if there had been only ten righteous in the city (Gen. 18:20-32). God allowed Abraham to continue because although Abraham, in his ignorance of the number of righteous in Sodom, could not have known the impossibility of his petition, it would have been in God's character to spare Sodom if there *had* been fifty righteous. This tells us that it is all right to persist in prayer if the character of the petition is within the character of God.

Importunity proves and establishes earnestness. The word for *importunity* can mean "shamelessness." The earnestness of the Capernaum nobleman (John 4:46-54) obtained through persistence what he asked. Peter's release from prison followed a prayer by the church which was made for him "fervently," which is literally "stretched-outedly" (Acts 12:5).

The promises Jesus gave concerning prayer were limitless. His emphasis was on the human activity—ask and receive, seek and find, knock and watch the door open. The implication is that God reacts favorably to the earnestness of His people. There can be no limitation on the divine ability to perform or the divine good will to give. If there is a limitation, it will be on the human imagination or faith. The imagination may be limited by a small conception of God's nature and resources, by a lack of understanding concerning the goodness of God, or by any number of spiritual disabilities. Faith may be limited by inadequate knowledge of the Word of God, by spiritual blindness, and sometimes by inexperience. Much that is experienced in daily living tends to dull spiritual imagination and faith. Jesus challenged us out of the quagmire of unbelief by giving promises that cannot be bound by human conception; we may ask "whatever" or "anything" (John 14:13-14).

Jesus attached a special condition and a special significance to one of His promises. If two or three are gathered in His name, He is in their midst, and the Father will do anything they agree to ask. My wife and I discovered the enormous potential of truly unified prayer during the dark days of her chemotherapy for cancer. As God united our spirits with His through the agonizing search to discover His purposes, we found our own spirits knit together in the tightest agreement we had ever known—agreement with His intentions, identity with His holiness, and mutuality in our life purposes. Although we had always practiced family devotions, the joy in our mutual prayer increased dramatically. And so did the dimensions of our prayer life together! As the bond grew tighter, our faith increased, and our prayers were answered in dimensions we had never known. We prayed when my wife developed shingles; all symptoms disappeared in three days. On another occasion we prayed for a computer. Without any knowledge of our needs or our prayer, a businessman in our city provided the funds for a computer. We discovered a principle: bonding in faith increases faith; the closer the bond, the more powerful the prayer.

The life of Jesus was singular in His emphasis on prayer. Having emptied Himself of His prerogatives as God (Phil. 2:6), He functioned as other human beings must function, through prayer. His power derived from prayer (Mark 9:29). On at least eleven different occasions, He taught on prayer. His teaching on prayer began in the early part of His Galilean ministry, in the Sermon on the Mount, and continued throughout His career; the night before He died He was still teaching on prayer. His example and His teaching are the greatest encouragement to prayer in the Bible.

PERSONAL LEARNING ACTIVITY 5

Read Matthew 18:19-20. These verses teach the value of praying in unity with others. Why do you think it is helpful to pray with others? _First of all there is as if were more power when two or more agree (example, Knights of C task_

Have you had a meaningful experience praying with another person? Describe that experience below. _No_

Notes
1. Marcus Rainsford, *Our Lord Prays for His Own: Thoughts on John 17* (Chicago: Moody Press, 1950), 40.

Chapter 3

The Holy Spirit—

Our Helper in Prayer

The Holy Spirit—the Indwelling Presence of Christ
The Holy Spirit and the Teaching and Purposes of Christ
The Holy Spirit and the Will of God
The Holy Spirit—Guide and Helper

One of the exciting aspects of learning a language is the discovery that certain ideas are peculiar to a given language and cannot be adequately translated into another. It requires much experience for English speakers to distinguish between *conocer* and *saber* ("to know") in Spanish, but a native speaker easily uses the two verbs correctly and would never confuse the two rather different concepts. As I was learning Japanese many years ago, I was thrilled to discover that certain ideas important in the Japanese mentality are not "thinkable" in English; I could think thoughts I had never thought before!

The same limitation applies to the different areas of human experience within the confines of any given language. I could describe musical phenomena in scientific language, but if I limit my description to the vocabulary of science alone, I will leave out some of the most important aspects of what music really is. A color-blind person might understand the mechanism of the light spectrum and perhaps even the structuring of cone cells in the eye that receive the various levels of the spectrum, but any three-year-old will *know* red and green in a way that the color-blind person does not.

Paul tells us that human beings have this same difficulty

thinking in spiritual terms: "A natural man does not accept the things of the Spirit of God; for they are foolishness to him, and he cannot understand them, because they are spiritually appraised" (1 Cor. 2:14). For this reason, all our attempts to explain a mystery as great as the Trinity are frustrated by language itself. For example, when we describe the functions of the Persons of the Trinity, we sometimes do an injustice to our understanding of the unity of the Godhead.

Scripture does not assume that it is necessary to understand these mysteries. It is more important to *know* God than it is to understand God. God was revealed in the Old Testament basically as One, but implicit through that revelation were indications of His plurality. Jesus did not repeal the faith of Israel that God is One but emphasized it (Mark 12:29-30). Throughout the New Testament the fact that God is One is assumed. Yet, in the New Testament the functions of the three Persons of the Trinity are presented. The New Testament writers saw no conflict in this emphasis on the three Persons of the Trinity and the unity of God as One.

Thus, the Third Person of the Trinity may properly be called the Holy Spirit, the "Spirit of Jesus Christ" (Phil. 1:19), or the "'Spirit of the Lord'" (Acts 5:9). He is the "Spirit of Christ" (Rom. 8:9), and yet Christ sent Him from the Father (John 15:26), just as Christ identified Himself with the Father (John 10:30; 14:9-11), and yet the Father sent Christ (John 6:38). The Holy Spirit will perform as Jesus performed, think as Jesus thinks, and plead as Jesus pleads. His present work is an exact continuation of the work of Christ.

The Holy Spirit—the Indwelling Presence of Christ

This is the Spirit which Jesus promised the disciples. He told them that the Spirit would indwell them: "'I will ask the Father, and He will give you another Helper, that He may be with you forever; that is the Spirit of truth, whom the world cannot receive, because it does not behold Him or know Him, but you know Him because He abides with you, and will be in you'" (John 14:16-17). Since the Holy Spirit dwells in the believer, the very body of the believer is the temple of the Holy Spirit (1 Cor. 6:19).

Yet after stating the promise in such a way that the Spirit was "'another Helper,'" Christ immediately identified Himself with the Spirit: "'I will not leave you as orphans; I will come to you'" (John 14:18). The Holy Spirit is the indwelling presence of Christ for every believer.

This indwelling Spirit also sanctifies (1 Pet. 1:2), and that, too, is the will and work of Christ (John 17:19; 1 Cor. 1:30). God expressed His love in sending the Son (1 John 4:10); God poured out His love through the Holy Spirit in the hearts of those justified by faith (Rom. 5:5). The work of Christ and the work of the Holy Spirit alike are pure expressions of all that God is and all that He intends for His people.

The Holy Spirit is indispensable to the prayer life of a Christian. We have our access to the Father through Christ (Eph. 2:18). Access to any throne is only through the strictest protocol; admission to the throne of the universe is available only through Christ. Our access to the Father is through Christ and is made real by the Spirit who lives within us. Spiritual prayer, prayer that is effective, is prayer led by the Holy Spirit.

The Holy Spirit and the Teaching and Purposes of Christ
The Holy Spirit makes the teaching and purposes of Christ, including prayer, real to the believer. The disciples knew that it was *Christ's* purposes for them that must be accomplished in their lives. They had learned much from Christ, but there was much yet to learn. Jesus told them, "'I

have many more things to say to you, but you cannot bear them now'" (John 16:12). He had assured them only moments before, "'The Helper, the Holy Spirit, whom the Father will send in My name, He will teach you all things, and bring to your remembrance all that I said to you'" (John 14:26). The departure of Christ need not threaten the loss of what they had learned; the Holy Spirit would restore it to memory and would bring new understandings which would harmonize with those of Christ. The revelation would be completed: "'When He, the Spirit of truth, comes, He will guide you into all the truth'" (John 16:13). Just as Christ did not work independently, on His own initiative (John 5:30), so the Spirit "will not speak on His own initiative, but whatever He hears, He will speak; and He will disclose to you what is to come" (John 16:13). Christ revealed the nature and will of the Father; the Holy Spirit will continue to reveal the teaching and purposes of Christ.

One of Christ's temptations had been to submit Himself to Satan, the prince of this world, in order to have "the kingdoms of the world, and their glory" (Matt. 4:8). Jesus later cautioned the disciples, "'I am not of this world'" (John 8:23), and He stated in His high-priestly prayer that the disciples themselves were given Him "'out of the world'" (John 17:6). Twice later in the same prayer He declared that they were "'not of the world'" (vv. 14,16). Paul said, "Now we have received, not the spirit of the world, but the Spirit who is from God, that we might know the things freely given to us by God, which things we also speak, not in words taught by human wisdom, but in those taught by the Spirit, combining spiritual thoughts with spiritual words" (1 Cor. 2:12-13). Whatever the Spirit taught them, it would not contradict what they had learned but would continue in the same vein as that which Christ had taught. It would be in the Spirit of Christ, and it would fulfill all that Christ started.

The Holy Spirit and the Will of God

Jesus had taught the disciples to pray "'Thy will be done.'" Evidently they did not fully understand how serious this plea should be, for later James, John, and their mother Salome approached Jesus with a request that was unanswerable at that time. They asked that they, James and John, sit on the right hand of the Lord in His kingdom. The error in their request was one which has caused difficulty for Christians throughout history. Their petition involved things they could not understand. Jesus explained, "'You do not know what you are asking for.'" They wanted positions of honor, but Jesus asked, in turn, another question that revealed a necessary consequence of such honor: "'Are you able to drink the cup that I am about to drink?'" (Matt. 20:22). Jesus wanted them to understand the implications of their request. This request angered the other disciples, and it demonstrated an ignorance of what constituted real greatness in the kingdom, as Jesus pointed out in verses 26-28.

It is encouraging to see that this kind of mistake early in life need not persist, for it was this same John who could write with joyous assurance, after much experience and many years, "This is the confidence which we have before Him, that, if we ask anything according to His will, He hears us" (1 John 5:14). In the course of his life after Matthew 20, John had learned to pray, "'Thy will be done,'" just as he had been taught, and sometime late in the same century, he recorded the assurance of prayer in God's will being answered.

The will of God was one of Jesus' major concerns. As a boy, He "had to be in the things of His Father" (a more literal translation of Luke 2:49). Early in His career, before the start of the Galilean ministry, He told some of His disciples, "'My food is to do the will of Him who sent Me, and to accomplish His work'" (John 4:34). Later, in a controversy over the sabbath, He claimed, "'My judgment is just, because I do not seek My own will, but the will of Him who sent Me'" (John 5:30). Some time after that He told a group in Capernaum, "'I have come down from heaven, not to do My own will, but the will of Him who sent Me" (John 6:38). Finally, at the end of His life, He could claim that He had accomplished the work which the Father had given Him to do (John 17:4). Even in Gethsemane, Jesus accepted the cup because it was the will of God (Matt. 26:39,42). The will of God was of such importance to Him that the author of Hebrews 10:7 saw in Psalm 40:7-8 a messianic utterance: "Then I said, 'Behold, I come; in the scroll of the book it is written of me; I delight to do Thy will, O my God; thy Law is within my heart.'"

Significantly, Jesus' devotion to the will of God became a major concern of His followers. John's confidence in prayers according to God's will (1 John 5:14) is also emphasized in 1 John 3:22. Jesus' half-brother James learned to govern his conversation by God's will (Jas. 4:15). God's will was of major importance to Peter. He stated that doing right, in the will of God, would silence the ignorance of foolish men (1 Pet. 2:15). Those who suffer according to the will of God should entrust their souls to God's faithfulness to do what is right (1 Pet. 4:19), and pastors should function voluntarily, according to the will of God (1 Pet. 5:2). Running throughout the writings of Paul is a recurrent theme of seeking and performing the will of God. Paul's actions were dependent on the will of God (Rom. 1:10; Acts 13:2; 16:6; 20:23). Paul even persuaded others to accept the will of God (Acts 21:14).

It is God's Holy Spirit who helps us understand the will of God. The psalmist sang, "Teach me to do Thy will, for Thou art my God; let Thy good Spirit lead me on level ground" (Ps. 143:10). The church in Antioch knew the will of God through the Holy Spirit: "While they were ministering to the Lord and fasting, the Holy Spirit said, 'Set apart for Me Barnabas and Saul for the work to which I have called them'" (Acts 13:2). Note that the Holy Spirit had *already* called Barnabas and Saul. The Holy Spirit forbade Paul to go into Asia (Acts 16:6)—a prohibition which rerouted the gospel into Europe. As he bade goodbye to the church in Ephesus, he stated that the Holy Spirit had testified to him about the bonds and afflictions awaiting him (Acts 20:23). It was Paul himself who wrote that the things of God can be known only through the Spirit of God:

For to us God revealed them [the things God has prepared for those who love Him] through the Spirit; for the Spirit searches all things, even the depths of God. For who among men knows the thoughts of a man except the spirit of the man, which is in him? Even so the thoughts of God no one knows except the Spirit of God (1 Cor. 2:10-11).

How can we know the will of God? The Bible, inspired by the Holy Spirit, is one source of revelation: "All Scripture is inspired by God and profitable for teaching, for reproof, for correction, for training in righteousness, that the man of God may be adequate, equipped for every good work" (2 Tim. 3:16-17). The psalmist declared that the testimony of the Lord made wise the simple and the commandment of the Lord enlightened the eyes (Ps. 19:7-8). The Bible reveals the kinds of thoughts God thinks, as they concern us, and the patterns those thoughts follow.

We may also know the will of God by prayer. Paul assured the Colossian church, "We have not ceased to pray for you and to ask that you may be filled with the knowledge of His will in all spiritual wisdom and understanding" (Col. 1:9). The prayer life of Jesus is the most convincing proof in the Bible of the work of the Holy Spirit in revealing God's will.

"Full of the Holy Spirit" (Luke 4:1), He was "led up by the Spirit" to His temptation (Matt. 4:1). After the temptation, He returned to Galilee "in the power of the Spirit" (Luke 4:14). He cast out demons by the Spirit of God (Matt. 12:28). It is He, whose earthly life was so totally controlled by the Spirit of God, who also prayed habitually. He prayed in times of decision (the choosing of the twelve), and He prayed in times of crisis (Gethsemane).

However, we cannot pray for the Spirit's direction unless we are willing to do God's will. Jesus repeatedly emphasized the importance of the human will and of openness to hear from God. He told the Pharisees, "'Why do you not understand what I am saying? It is because you cannot hear My word'" (John 8:43). Unwillingness to accept God's revelation blinded them. Unwillingness is deliberate; Jesus, quoting from Isaiah 6:10, said that the Jews had "'closed their eyes'" (Matt. 13:15).

Later Jesus would declare, "'He who is of God hears the words of God'" (John 8:47). Hearing is a live option; Jesus often invited, "'He who has ears to hear, let him hear'" (Mark 4:9). Jesus used the tender figure of the shepherd and the sheep to describe how naturally His "sheep" could hear His voice:

To him [the shepherd] the doorkeeper opens, and the sheep hear his voice, and he calls his own sheep by name, and leads them out. When he puts forth all his own, he goes before them, and the sheep follow him because they know his voice. And a stranger they simply will not follow, but will flee from him, because they do not know the voice of strangers (John 10:3-5).

He told the disciples, "'Blessed are your eyes, because they see; and your ears, because they hear'" (Matt. 13:16).

God is willing to give wisdom liberally; all we have to do is ask (Jas. 1:5). Asking involves a willing spirit. It is a willing spirit which enables us to recognize divine teaching: "'If any man is willing to do His [God's] will, he shall know of the teaching, whether it is of God, or whether I speak from Myself'" (John 7:17). To "hear" from the Holy Spirit what God's will is, it is absolutely essential that we come to prayer desiring God's will, asking for God's will, and being disposed to carry out God's will if it involves action.

The Holy Spirit—Guide and Helper

The Holy Spirit is the believer's guide and helper in prayer. People have sensed a need for guidance and help in discerning the will of God throughout history. Long ago Jeremiah pleaded with God, "I know, O Lord, that a man's way is not in himself; nor is it in a man who walks to direct his steps. Correct me, O Lord, but with justice; not with Thine anger, lest Thou bring me to nothing" (Jer. 10:23-24). With the advent of the Christian message and the indwelling of the Spirit of God, Jeremiah's ancient plea found its answer, an answer available to every believer.

In the same way the Spirit also helps our weakness; for we do not know how to pray as we should, but the Spirit Himself intercedes for us with groanings too deep for words; and He who searches the hearts knows what the mind of the Spirit is, because He intercedes for the saints according to the will of God (Rom. 8:26-27).

The word *help* is the same word that Martha used in Luke 10:40 when she asked Jesus to require Mary's help in the kitchen. The help of the Holy Spirit is useful for accomplishing specific tasks. The specific weakness He helps in this case is our inadequate knowledge of how to pray. He helps with unutterable groanings, with depth of meaning to the divine mind far beyond where human language can venture.

The intercession is "for"—on behalf of—the saints and is always in perfect accordance with the will of God. The Spirit is translating our awkward prayers into the noble and high intentions of God Himself, who gives only good and perfect gifts (Jas. 1:17).

PERSONAL LEARNING ACTIVITY 6

Read Romans 8:26-27. In the space provided, write what you believe the writer meant when he said that the Spirit "intercedes for us with groanings too deep for words."

_____

_____

_____

_____

The name of the Holy Spirit in the Lord's last discourse is often translated "Helper" (John 14:26; 15:26; 16:7). Here the word *Helper* means "one called alongside," that is, to help.

The Holy Spirit serves as our guide into all truth (John 16:13). His very name is "'Spirit of truth'" (John 15:26; 16:13), and it is *all* truth He leads us into. There is no limit to how much of the Spirit's help we can have; John the Baptist assured us that Christ gives the Spirit without measure (John 3:34).

Since the Holy Spirit knows the will of God and is our guide and helper in prayer, it is important that our minds, lives, hearts, purposes, and activities be filled with Him. If someone says, "That speaker is full of his subject," most of us understand what he means. If I say a boy is "full of football," most people understand that football permeates his thinking and talk in school, at the table, at play, and in church. He has placed football ahead of everything else, and football will dominate all that he does. We are commanded to be continually filled with the Spirit (Eph. 5:18). Our orientation to everything in life is to be spiritual. If we are filled with the Spirit, the mind and purpose of the Spirit will take precedence over every attitude. The Spirit will govern our thinking, will be the major influence in every decision, and will be observable in all our actions.

We are to pray in the Spirit; this will not be possible unless we are filled with the Spirit. "With all prayer and petition pray at all times in the Spirit" (Eph. 6:18); the key word is *all*—"all in prayer," "all times"—that is, every petition, every prayer proceeds from the mind of the Spirit, not from selfish motives or self-serving ends. Jude makes this same lesson graphic by first giving the opposite of spiritual praying (often we can understand a concept by thinking of its opposite): "These are the ones who cause divisions, worldly-minded, devoid of the Spirit" (Jude 19). Jude then piles up phrases describing the accompaniment of praying in the Spirit: "But you, beloved, building yourselves up on your most holy faith; praying in the Holy Spirit; keep yourselves in the love of God, waiting anxiously for the mercy of our Lord Jesus Christ to eternal life" (Jude 20-21).

Praying in the Spirit does not rule out praying with the mind. The mind provides our prayers with precise meaning. Praying in generalities obtains answers "in general." It is not enough to pray, "Be with us," for God is always with us; we need to ask for the specific purpose of God's presence in our lives.

The mind is an instrument for ordering our prayers. The

psalmist speaks of daily laying his requests before God (Ps. 5:3). Still, God's power is unleashed through the Spirit; the word of the Lord to Zerubbabel was, "'Not by might, nor by power, but by My Spirit'" (Zech. 4:6). We need not fear mindless abandon if God's Spirit is in control. Praying which pleases God is neither in mindless spirit nor spiritless mind, but rather it is prayer in which the mind is tuned to the frequency of the Holy Spirit, who is in control.

The Holy Spirit is available to us, is in us, and is alongside us. He glorifies Christ, enlightens our minds, opens to us the will of God, guides us, and helps our prayers, both as we utter them on earth and as they are interpreted in heaven. There is no accomplishing the work of Christ without the prayer-help of the Holy Spirit.

Chapter 4

The Ways

People
Pray

Prayer of Adoration Is a Form of Prayer
Prayer of Intercession Is a Form of Prayer
Prayer of Petition Is a Form of Prayer
Prayer of Repentance Is a Form of Prayer
Prayer for Deliverance Is a Form of Prayer

Prayer is fellowship with God (1 John 1:3) and grows out of a relationship with God so multifaceted that no single form of prayer exhausts all the potential of that relationship. The Bible provides us with multiple pictures of our relationship with God. Sometimes our relationship is that of a father and child, sometimes of a master and servant, at other times of an older brother and other family members, of a teacher and disciple, and of a leader and follower. This is one reason why the Old Testament gives us so many names for God (the Almighty, the Holy One, Rock, Refuge) and the New Testament supplies additional names for Christ (Bread, Door, Shepherd, Friend, High Priest). In the same way that we cannot exhaust all that God is with human words, we cannot limit our dialogue with Him to one kind of prayer.

There are many kinds of prayer because there are many aspects of our relationship with God. At times His greatness will be the primary focus, as, for example, when that which is created praises the Creator. At times His beneficence will be primary, when we speak gratefully to our Benefactor. In time of need, we are suppliant, and God is Source. The various aspects of His limitless nature alternately move in and out of our vision as we need His mercy, His provision, His protection, His strength, or simply His smile. People pray in many different ways for many different reasons. The Model Prayer, often referred to as the Lord's Prayer, provides us with an outline that covers most of the major directions prayer will take.

Prayer of Adoration Is a Form of Prayer

The Model Prayer begins in worship, with a recognition of God's nature and identity. He is, above all and first of all, Father, and He is spiritual—" 'who art in heaven.' " That He is in heaven does not mean that He is distant from us on earth, but that He is different from the world; the God we pray to is spiritual.

Jesus said we are to worship Him in spirit and in truth (John 4:24). This difficult concept may be understood best by comparing it to its opposite. The opposite of worship *in spirit* is anything which will limit God to time or space as our physical senses perceive them.

There is no "correct" hour of prayer, although it is helpful to order our day so that, for example, we begin the day with prayer. There is also no fixed place to which prayer is limited, although certain places are important to the believer in praying—a place alone, the family devotions, or the assembling of believers. What is the opposite of worship *in truth*? The opposite is praying in meaningless formula, in insincerity, in falsity of doctrine or attitude.

We are to hallow or recognize as holy the name or the identity of God. But this is only a beginning. The Model Prayer is suggestive, not exhaustive. The Bible is full of other kinds of adoration. We worship God for all of His attributes, and in the Bible, holiness is always given precedence. Again and again in the great encounters with God, great people of God saw first His holiness—Moses (Ex. 3:5), Isaiah (Isa. 6:3), and Peter (Luke 5:8). Recognition of His holiness formed an introductory part of the profound prayers of Hannah (1 Sam. 2:2) and Mary (Luke 1:49).

Biblical praise manifests many other attributes of God also. The psalmist praised Him for His majesty and greatness (Ps. 104:1; see also Isa. 9:6), His splendor and strength (Ps. 96:6), His character (Ps. 18:2-3), His glory (Ps. 19:1), and the joy of His presence (Ps. 84). Many of the psalms are songs of pure praise (Pss. 103; 106; 111; 112; 113; 117; 135; 146; 147; 148). Some are hymns to His majesty (Pss. 8; 19; 24; 29; 48; 50; 76; 93; 97), and some are joyful expressions of abandon (Pss. 47; 66; 81; 148). In the New Testament, Paul sometimes concluded his arguments with a doxology:

> *Oh, the depth of the riches both of the wisdom and knowledge of God! How unsearchable are His judgments and unfathomable His ways! . . . For from Him and through Him and to Him are all things. To Him be the glory forever. Amen. (Rom. 11:33-36).*

Many of the biblical expressions of praise treat at length the creative power of God. The main theme of Psalm 104 is expressed in verse 24: "O Lord, how many are Thy works! In wisdom Thou hast made them all; the earth is full of Thy possessions." The rest of the psalm rapturously describes the Lord moving through His possessions (vv. 2-4), creating them (vv. 5-9), and maintaining them (vv. 10-32). Creation is also a major theme in many other psalms (Pss. 8; 19; 24; 50; 66; 93; 97; 98), and praise for creation and in creation assumes cosmic proportions in the last three psalms of the Psalter (Pss. 148-150).

Another important form of praise in the Old Testament is a recounting of history with a view to God's role in it. Exodus 15 is a tribute to God's supernatural actions in delivering Israel out of Egypt. Several of the psalms tell of Israel's history as God acted on her behalf (Pss. 78; 105; 106; 114; 135; 136). These are important because Israel so quickly forgot what God did for her. Perhaps if she had remembered, she would not have complained in the desert or would not have gone after false gods.

These Old Testament "praise-histories" prepared the way for a similar type of praise in the New Testament as believers praised God for what He had done for them in Christ. Peter extolled God as a Father who acted:

> *Blessed be the God and Father of our Lord Jesus Christ, who according to His great mercy has caused us to be born again to a living hope through the resurrection of Jesus Christ from the dead, to obtain an inheritance which is imperishable and undefiled and will not fade away, reserved in heaven for you (1 Pet. 1:3-4).*

Paul exclaimed also, "Blessed be the God and Father of our Lord Jesus Christ, who has blessed us with every spiritual blessing in the heavenly places in Christ" (Eph. 1:3) and continued with a threefold doxology that indicated the praiseworthiness of the grace of each of the Persons of the Trinity (of the Father in Eph. 1:6, of the Son in Eph. 1:12, and of the Holy Spirit in Eph. 1:14).

Jesus began the Model Prayer with an acknowledgment of the position and the nature of God. This beginning places things in perspective. This perspective is basic to true prayer. Worship is the human appreciation of and adoration of God, and it places all else we pray in proper relationship and perspective.

Closely related to praise in the Bible is thanksgiving. Praise and thanksgiving are often mentioned together in the psalms: "Praise the Lord! Oh give thanks to the Lord, for He is good; for His lovingkindness is everlasting" (Ps. 106:1). The psalmist said that praise and thanksgiving would declare the character of God: "It is good to give thanks to the Lord, and to sing praises to Thy name, O Most High; to declare Thy lovingkindness in the morning, and Thy faithfulness by night" (Ps. 92:1-2).

Through Moses, God gave a commandment that when the offering of firstfruits was brought to the Lord, the Jewish citizen was to pray, " 'Now behold, I have brought the first of the produce of the ground which Thou, O Lord hast given me.' " The commandment continues:

> *"You shall set it down before the Lord your God, and worship before the Lord your God; and you and the Levite and the alien who is among you shall rejoice in all the good which the Lord your God has given you and your household" (Deut. 26:10-11).*

This is what thanksgiving is about—it declares our understanding of what is good, we rejoice in it and acknowledge its source. Thanksgiving is rejoicing in what God declares to be good and is important because it establishes our relationship to our Source.

The word *all* becomes important when the Bible talks about thanksgiving. Many people assume that we thank God only for what we perceive to be blessings. Such an attitude obviously grows out of and leads to materialism. Paul wrote, "In everything give thanks; for this is God's will for you in Christ Jesus" (1 Thess. 5:18). One can only give thanks *in* all things, *for* all things, if he is convinced that "God causes all things to work together for good to those who love God, to those who are called according to His purpose" (Rom. 8:28).

The attitude of thanksgiving is also to permeate our petitions: "Be anxious for nothing, but in everything by prayer and supplication with thanksgiving let your requests be made known to God" (Phil. 4:6; see also Col. 4:2). The result of this attitude will be an incomprehensible peace (Phil 4:7). Paul's own expressions of gratitude usually included such words as *all, always,* and *everything* (Phil. 1:3;

Col. 1:3; Col. 3:17; 1 Thess. 1:2; 2 Thess. 1:3). Even in the Old Testament, thanksgiving was to be total, of all the being, for all God's works. Four times in the psalms, the psalmist declared, "I will give thanks to the Lord with all my heart" (Pss. 9:1; 86:12; 111:1; 138:1). In the first of these, the parallel consequent phrase declares, "I will tell of *all* Thy wonders."

Prayer of Intercession Is a Form of Prayer
After the hallowing of God's name, the Model Prayer takes us to bringing the kingdom and accomplishing God's will. The New Testament is full of intercessory prayer that does just that. Intercessory prayer, or prayer on behalf of others, reaches its highest power and its highest goal when it is intended to bring the kingdom and accomplish the will of God. This, in fact, is the purpose of all prayer—to accomplish the will of God. The greatest example, not only of intercessory prayer, but of prayer to bring God's kingdom, is Jesus' own prayer in John 17. Just as He prayed for Peter (Luke 22:32), He prayed for His disciples in John 17, and in verse 20 He indicated that He was praying for all disciples in all times.

Christ is our example in intercessory prayer. The work He began on earth He continues through all time. He is now appearing in the presence of God for us (Heb. 9:24) and always lives to make intercession for those who draw near to God (Heb. 7:25). One of the most poignant expressions of the loving and propitious attitude of our Intercessor was developed by Paul:

> *Who will bring a charge against God's elect? God is the one who justifies; who is the one who condemns? Christ Jesus is He who died, yes, rather who was raised, who is at the right hand of God, who also intercedes for us (Rom. 8:33-34).*

Believers also are taught to pray for one another. Mutual intercession was widely practiced in the New Testament church. James commanded, "Therefore, confess your sins to one another, and pray for one another, so that you may be healed. The effective prayer of a righteous man can accomplish much" (Jas. 5:16). The prayer of the Jerusalem church for Peter in Acts 12:5 "accomplished much" in his release from prison. Paul requested the prayers of the Thessalonians (1 Thess. 5:25), and he even asked the Roman church "to strive together with me in your prayers to God for me" (Rom. 15:30). The word Paul used means "to strive with" and indicates that Paul expected them to be earnest in prayer for him.

The scope of the intercessory prayers recorded in the New Testament is almost inexhaustible. Paul prayed for the churches of his day—that they be spiritually enlightened (Eph. 1:15-20) and that they know the will of God, walk worthy of Him, bear fruit, and be strengthened (Col. 1:9-11; see also Phil. 1:9; 1 Thess. 3:10-13; and 2 Thess. 1:11). He prayed that they comprehend the love of Christ in order to be filled with the fullness of God (Eph. 3:14-19) and that their sanctification and preservation be complete (1 Thess. 5:23). Each of these prayers is so instructive that it merits extended study.

Paul also requested the prayers of his churches. He asked the Ephesians that they pray for him to have bold utterance (Eph. 6:19), and he asked the Colossians that they pray for him to speak with boldness and clarity (Col. 4:3-4). He requested the Thessalonians, "Pray for us that the word of the Lord may spread rapidly and be glorified . . . and that we may be delivered from perverse and evil men" (2 Thess. 3:1-2).

He was so confident in the power of their prayers that he associated his work with their prayers as a joint catalyst in accomplishing the will of God. He expected them to be thankful for the answers to their prayers for him: "You also joining in helping us through your prayers, that thanks may be given by many persons on our behalf for the favor bestowed upon us through the prayers of many" (2 Cor. 1:11). He expressed confidence that the prayers of the Philippian church would accomplish his deliverance from prison (Phil. 1:19).

PERSONAL LEARNING ACTIVITY 7

Intercessory prayer, prayer on behalf of others, is important for Christians. List the names of persons who need prayer for the reasons suggested. Pray for these individuals each day for a week.

_____ is physically sick. I will pray
     (name)
for him/her each day.

_____ has a family problem. I will
     (name)
pray for him/her each day.

_____ needs strength for Christian
     (name)
service. I will pray for him/her each day.

Prayer of Petition Is a Form of Prayer

The next request in the Model Prayer is "'Give us this day our daily bread.'" Not only are we encouraged to pray for one another, but we are told again and again that we may make personal petitions to the Lord. The prayers mentioned in the preceding section are sublimely spiritual in nature, but this petition involves everyday physical needs, indicating that the Lord considers our physical needs important enough to pray about. Petition is an important part of our prayer life.

In the Sermon on the Mount, Jesus taught us to ask, seek, and knock (Matt. 7:7-8). The numerous instances of requests to Christ for healing are examples of asking. Asking suggests dependence, as, for example, the dependence of a child upon his parents. Jesus, in fact, immediately after enjoining us to ask, gave the encouraging example of a father anxious to give good gifts to his son and indicated that the Heavenly Father was immeasurably more willing than an earthly father. Asking, therefore, suggests the humility of dependence on the part of the petitioner and willingness on the part of God.

Seeking suggests yearning, earnestness, and effort. Nicodemus was a seeker (John 3). Isaiah urged that we "seek the Lord while He may be found" (Isa. 55:6). Jesus told us to " 'seek first His kingdom and His righteousness' " (Matt. 6:33), and Paul phrased it, "Keep seeking the things above" (Col. 3:1). We are not to seek only our own good, but that of our neighbor (1 Cor. 10:24).

Knocking suggests persistence or, as the Bible puts it, importunity. Jacob's night-long wrestling with God is an example of persistence (Gen. 32:24-29). Strangely, the Bible speaks more of the Lord knocking on our door than of our knocking on His (Luke 12:36; Rev. 3:20); He is persistent in His wooing of us. Since the word Jesus used for "knock" is that which is normally used of a knock to gain admission, the suggestion is that the kingdom contains many opportunities to which Christians may be admitted.

Jesus, therefore, was suggesting three attitudes which should permeate prayer—dependence, earnestness, and persistence. The pronouns in Matthew 7:7 are all plural; the potential of prayer with others has yet to be explored by the home and the church. Interestingly enough, the assurance of God's answer is stated in the singular, and it is comprehensive: " 'For every one who asks receives, and he who seeks finds, and to him who knocks it shall be opened'" (Matt. 7:8).

One of the most important of the biblical petitions is the frequently repeated prayer for strength in God's service. The most eloquent of several examples of this is given in Acts 4:24-31. It may have been spoken by Peter, but the church agreed "with one accord." The prayer began with a quotation from Psalm 2, a messianic psalm, equating the resistance of the Jerusalem priests to the new Christian movement with that of the rulers "against the Lord and against His Anointed" in the psalm. One of the reasons for the rapid expansion of the New Testament church was the frequency of the repetition of this prayer for boldness of proclamation and strength in God's service (Eph. 3:16; Eph. 6:19; Col. 1:11; Col. 4:3; 2 Thess. 2:17).

Petition is to be presented without anxiety and with thanksgiving (Phil. 4:6); Paul assured the Philippian church that God would supply all needs "according to His riches in glory in Christ Jesus" (Phil. 4:19). The result of this kind of prayer will be that "the peace of God, which surpasses all comprehension, shall guard your hearts and your minds in Christ Jesus" (Phil. 4:7). The reasonableness of this is seen in the presence of the God of peace in the lives of those who obey Paul's injunctions (Phil. 4:9).

PERSONAL LEARNING ACTIVITY 8

The writer says that Jesus suggested three attitudes in Matthew 7:7 which should characterize our praying. Beside each attitude write why you feel it is important.

dependence: _____

earnestness: _____

Can I take a step according ynat his guidance.

persistence: _____

_____

_____

Prayer of Repentance Is a Form of Prayer

After the prayer for daily sustenance, Jesus told us to ask for forgiveness of our sins. For the Christian, this is not asking for a legal cancellation of sin, of course, for the cross cancels the legal debt of our sin. But constant agreement with God about the nature of sin is the only way we can maintain fellowship with Him in His holiness.

John wrote, "If we confess our sins, He is faithful and righteous to forgive us our sins and to cleanse us from all unrighteousness" (1 John 1:9). The word for "confess" literally means "to say the same thing" and implies agreement with another. Confession is not just admitting our sins to God; He never needs information. Rather, confession is aligning ourselves in attitude with Him. Sin grieves *us* in our new nature in the same way (but not to the same extent) that it grieves God. When I sin, I do not tell God, "I admit that I sinned," but rather I tell Him that I agree with Him about the nature of my action and, in doing so, align myself with His attitude toward it.

When we pray to God, we should pray only in accord with what we know of His character, and this is in accord with Jesus' command that we ask for forgiveness "'as we also have forgiven our debtors.'" God's mercy is limitless, and Jesus answered Peter's question about our limit on forgiveness by saying that we should forgive "'up to seventy times seven.'" There must be no limit to our forgiveness, just as there is no limit on God's. Jesus illustrated His command to Peter with the story of the slave forgiven by his king who would not himself forgive others (Matt. 18:23-35). We are not to be like the slave; we are to be like the king in the parable. Jesus' own example is like that of the king. On the cross Jesus prayed, "'Father, forgive them; for they do not know what they are doing'" (Luke 23:34). We are to have the mind of Christ (Phil. 2:5).

Many Christians associate forgiveness with feelings and struggle to change inner feelings. Forgiveness is an action, legal in nature. The example of Stephen is instructive. Compare his dying prayer to that of Jesus. As Stephen was dying, he prayed, "'Lord, do not hold this sin against them!'" (Acts 7:60). Paul wrote, "Never take your own revenge, beloved, but leave room for the wrath of God, for it is written, 'Vengeance is Mine, I will repay, says the Lord'" (Rom. 12:19, quoting Deut. 32:35).

Forgiveness, then, is simply placing all aspects of our case in the hands of God, turning it over to God, as Stephen did; we give it to our Defender, who says that revenge is His own prerogative. It frees God to work in the lives of those who hurt us, according to His wisdom and His pleasure rather than our changing whims. It is likely that the conversion of Saul of Tarsus, who watched Stephen die, had at least some root in Stephen's remarkable prayer. Much of Jesus' teaching on forgiveness was in connection with prayer. It is in prayer, in fellowship with God, that we demonstrate best His character, as Stephen did.

It is as imperative that we accept forgiveness from God as it is that we forgive others. The Bible again and again gives a picture of infinite divine forgiveness, sometimes with graphic language and picturesque figures to help us understand the greatness of God's mercy. Micah said that God will "cast all their sins into the depths of the sea" when He forgives them (Mic. 7:19). Isaiah described it as wiping out our transgressions and quoted the Lord as saying that He would not remember our sins (Isa. 43:25). He quoted a writing of Hezekiah: "Thou hast cast all my sins behind Thy back" (Isa. 38:17).

But supremely it was the New Testament which gave us the most adequate picture of perfect cancellation of forgiven sin. The writer of Hebrews asked,

> *For if the blood of goats and bulls and the ashes of a heifer sprinkling those who have been defiled, sanctify for the cleansing of the flesh, how much more will the blood of Christ, who through the eternal Spirit offered Himself without blemish to God, cleanse your conscience from dead works to serve the living God? (Heb. 9:13-14)*

A young woman once called me in deep remorse over sin in her life. She believed in the forgiveness of God yet felt unclean. I asked her, "If the blood of Christ is what cleanses you, how clean would you be?"

God's forgiveness is absolute; all His actions, like His attributes, are absolutes. The Keil and Delitzsch translation of Lamentations 3:22-23 gives a picture of mercy so unfailing that it is ever new: "[It is a sign of] the mercies of Jahveh that we are not consumed, for His compassions fail not; [they are] new every morning: great is Thy faithfulness."[1] Repeatedly, God's mercies or lovingkindnesses are described as infinite or as multitudinous (Isa. 63:7; Ps. 89:2), and the measure of God's forgiveness is not our feelings but His great compassion (Ps. 51:1). God's compassions are renewed daily!

Newness is the law of the kingdom, and *new* is one of the most important words in the New Testament. Newness characterizes not only God's compassions, but our walk in newness of life (Rom. 6:4). Paul encouraged all Christians of history with his word, "Therefore if any man is in Christ, he is a new creature; the old things passed away; behold, new things have come" (2 Cor. 5:17). Forgiven sin, the old, is in the past and is to be put there; it has passed away.

Prayer for Deliverance Is a Form of Prayer

After the plea for forgiveness in the Model Prayer comes a prayer for deliverance from evil. The word for "evil" here could be either neuter—evil in general—or masculine—that is, Satan. Jesus used this word in Matthew 13:19,38 to refer to Satan, as did Paul in Ephesians 6:16. In either case, the injunction to pray for deliverance from it implies that deliverance is the will of God and may be secured through prayer.

Our protection from temptation is important to Jesus. Later He Himself asked on our behalf this very petition: " 'I do not ask Thee to take them out of the world, but to keep them from the evil one'" (John 17:15). The same night He prayed this prayer, He urged the disciples to " 'pray that you may not enter into temptation'" (Luke 22:40). Repetition of the injunction lends weight to its importance.

The protection God gives is effective; John wrote about a sure confidence: "We know that no one who is born of God sins; but He [Christ] who was born of God keeps him and the evil one does not touch him" (1 John 5:18). Paul gave the same assurance: "The Lord is faithful, and He will strengthen and protect you from the evil one" (2 Thess. 3:3). He assured Timothy, "The Lord will deliver me from every evil deed, and will bring me safely to His heavenly kingdom" (2 Tim. 4:18). Peter echoed the same idea: "Then the Lord knows how to rescue the godly from temptation" (2 Pet. 2:9). The most decisive and unquestionable assurance of deliverance in the New Testament, after the injunction of Jesus, is Paul's rather bold statement:

No temptation has overtaken you but such as is common to man; and God is faithful, who will not allow you to be tempted beyond what you are able, but with the temptation will provide the way of

*escape also, that you may be able to endure it
(1 Cor. 10:13).*

The Christian may ask for general protection and safety. The names by which God is called in the Psalter—Shield, Fortress, Refuge—indicate an ancient, rocklike faith in God's keeping power. The writers of the Old Testament repeatedly assured us of safety and protection under Yahweh:

- *I have set the Lord continually before me; because He is at my right hand, I will not be shaken (Ps. 16:8, quoted by Peter in his Pentecost sermon, Acts 2:25).*
- *He will give His angels charge concerning you, to guard you in all your ways (Ps. 91:11).*
- *The Lord is your keeper; the Lord is your shade on your right hand (Ps. 121:5).*
- *Every word of God is tested; He is a shield to those who take refuge in Him (Prov. 30:5).*
- *For the eyes of the Lord move to and fro throughout the earth that He may strongly support those whose heart is completely His (2 Chron. 16:9; Hanani the seer was speaking to Asa when Asa refused to rely on the Lord).*

The forms suggested by the Model Prayer are limited only by our imagination and should be amplified by study of all the prayers of the Bible. In all of them, we identify with God and are being brought increasingly into His image. Whatever form we use, our hearts and minds remain in agreement with Him and His purposes, in all circumstances, and in all times. Prayer is fellowship with God and is successful only as it is in agreement with Him.

Notes
1. C. F. Keil and F. Delitzsch, *Commentary on the Old Testament in Ten Volumes* (Grand Rapids, MI: William B. Eerdmans Publishing Company, n.d.), VIII, 401.

Chapter 5

Questions

About
Prayer

The Scriptures and experience are intended to encourage us to pray, but many Christians feel a vague reluctance to pray. This reluctance may be rooted in uncertainties in their minds. Uncertainty is the enemy of faith. It is better to face our questions squarely, to accept the verdict of Scripture, and to move forward into the kind of prayer that pleases God and accomplishes His will.

If God Already Knows Everything, Why Should We Pray?

There can be no question that God knows everything. Certainly a loving Father would desire the fellowship, not the silence, of His children. The real questions, therefore, are what is prayer, and what does it do?

Of the beings of higher intelligence, the Bible names only two orders—humankind and angels. *That* the angels were created is quite clear (Neh. 9:6; Col. 1:16). Like humanity, they were made. The fact that they are spiritual in nature (Heb. 1:14) and powerful (Ps. 103:20) leads many people to believe that they are eternally superior to humanity in rank.

Nevertheless, the Bible pictures redeemed humanity as presently in training for a future reign which will be superior to all other revealed orders of creation. Ultimately we are to be superior in authority and rank to the angels themselves. It was Adam, not an angel, who was made in the image of God and granted dominion over animal life (Gen. 1:26), but Adam fell and spoiled God's plan for him. The second Adam, Jesus Christ, did not fall and, as representative Man, removed the curse of the law necessitated by the fall of the first Adam (Gal. 3:13). Christ accomplished the possibility of a return to "the image of the heavenly" for the human race (1 Cor. 15:49).

What is involved in the achievement of this second Adam? Even in their *present* earthly life, the authority of those followers who accept His new life exceeds all imagination. They are redeemed and forgiven (Eph. 1:7), born eternally of imperishable seed (1 Pet. 1:23), and are now children of God (Rom. 8:16). As such, they have the mind of Christ Himself (1 Cor. 2:16), are conformed to His image (Rom. 8:29), and therefore bear "the image of the heavenly" (1 Cor. 15:49). In this new and secure position, they bear a regal authority; Paul wrote the Corinthian church, "All things belong to you" (1 Cor. 3:22).

The *future* of this new humanity is even more exalted and noble. They are joint heirs with Christ, who is the heir of all things (Heb. 1:2), and will be glorified with Him (Rom. 8:17). They are to reign with Him (2 Tim. 2:12; see also Rom. 5:17; Luke 22:29-30; and Rev. 20:6) and therefore are the ultimate and cosmic nobility of eternity. It is somewhat frightening that they will also sit in judgment on angels (1 Cor. 6:3)—surely an awesome authority hardly conceivable at the present! So great is the destiny of children of God that creation is actually longing expectantly for the unveiling of the identity of the sons of God (Rom. 8:19)!

If you were God, bringing His children to that high state, how would you do it? The children of earthly kings around the world are trained in the ways of nobility from infancy. They participate in the privileges of royalty, learn the courtesies of the court, are trained in the interaction of various offices and authorities, study carefully the responsibilities of their present and future office, and assume such responsibilities as their age will allow. Their own relation to the ruling monarch is expected to be responsible. They are royal from birth and are expected to act like it.

Much of this description of children of earthly monarchs is consistent with the Bible's description of the nature and work of the future rulers of the universe. Our work is a royal work; we are actually workers together with God (2 Cor. 6:1). Our nature is like the Sovereign's; we are His children. It is His court, and the responsibilities are spelled out by His word.

Most important of all the work is spiritual work. Spiritual work can be accomplished only with spiritual methods, and the only mover in any spiritual project must be God Himself. How do we cooperate with God in this work? The answer is obviously prayer. This is why the Bible places so much emphasis on prayer. Prayer is an awesome, regal responsibility, carrying with it great accountability but also possibilities of vast accomplishment.

God could move on His own, as He did in creation and redemption. He can take the initiative. He needs no permission to act. And yet, dealing with His children, it was His wisdom to place them in a training ground appropriate to their learning processes. We are to govern; we exist in an environment containing spiritual elements hostile to His sovereignty. What else could be better training?

This is why in *everything* we are to present our requests with thanksgiving to God. Nothing is excluded, because all things affect the progress of the kingdom. Our work is large, and our faith operates across that part of God's sovereignty visible to us. The long list of things we should pray for in the Bible (for governors, for the churches, for boldness) brings the entire movement of humankind, government, churches, and the kingdom under the influence of our prayers.

God could move without our cooperation, but our cooperation is the method He uses to demonstrate His sovereignty. All power derives from God; He is the most powerful Agent in the universe. Prayer provides a way for us to cooperate with our all-powerful God.

God could work without prayer; some of His work was done unilaterally. The might, glory, and power of creation and redemption are beyond our comprehension; we could not have cooperated in them. Creation and redemption are uniquely a divine work, too grand for what we were made to be. But the governing of the universe and the management of the world we know are not beyond us. God has chosen to bring us in on that governing process because of our eternal work of reigning which is ahead of us.

At times we cannot see this grand picture because our minds become befuddled by our sins, blemishes, and various imperfections. We cannot see the forest for the trees, and we cannot see the trees for the moss, rocks, and grass. But the forest, the grand picture, is there. It is quite clear in Scripture.

So in prayer we ask. At times we get outside the bounds of His plan and ask for the wrong thing or ask from wrong motives. We must learn, and we can learn even from our mistakes. That is what we are now doing. How does a ruler rule? We have to go through God's process.

Sometimes we seek. But not all is appropriate for a spiritual kingdom or for a holy God. At times our seeking becomes groping because that is the only way we can learn to seek in the right manner. Sometimes we seem to stumble upon the right answer and delight in our progress.

At times we knock. Not all opportunities are proper for royalty, but many are, and, living as we are, with the mind of Christ, in the image of God, representing the interests of the one King, we delight when those noble and right opportunities open up before our earnest progress.

We do not pray to give God information. We pray because of who we are. It is the wise and holy decision of God Himself that the work of His kingdom be advanced through prayer. His choice of method is that we do that most important of all works. He uses us, directs us to pray rightly, and validates His work in us by kingdom progress. We cannot base our spiritual work on our material resources—our own money, strength, or talent. God does not need our resources; all things belong to Him (Ps. 50:7-12). We need to use all the resources available to us in the power of God Himself—His wisdom, His spiritual way, His will, His might (Zech. 4:6).

PERSONAL LEARNING ACTIVITY 9

Since God already knows everything about our lives and circumstances, why does He want us to pray? Write your answer in the space provided. _____

_____

_____

If People Are Free to Make Their Own Choices, What Good Does It Do to Pray for Others?

This presents us with the age-old problem of the balance of God's sovereignty with the free will of man. Quite unmistakably, Jesus affirmed:

> *You did not choose Me, but I chose you, and*
> *appointed you, that you should go and bear fruit,*
> *and that your fruit should remain, that whatever you*
> *ask of the Father in My name, He may give it to you*
> *(John 15:16).*

Yet He also invited, "Let the one who wishes take the water of life without cost" (Rev. 22:17). The biblical paradoxes usually open wider the doors of our understanding.

Each of the two statements is reinforced by numerous other references. Jesus clearly *chose* the twelve (Luke 6:13); the disciples' understanding of His prerogative to choose is shown in their prayer for Judas's replacement: "'Thou, Lord, who knowest the hearts of all men, show which one of these two Thou hast chosen'" (Acts 1:24). He told Ananias, as Ananias was doubting Saul of Tarsus, "'He is a chosen instrument of Mine'" (Acts 9:15). Yet the rich young ruler had complete freedom to choose his own will, to reject Christ (Matt. 19:22). The Bible unapologetically presents the elective freedom of God to choose whom He will; it also clearly leaves the choice of accepting or rejecting God to the individual.

There is a dynamic interplay between the will of God and the will of man that becomes like a divinely directed drama. The initiative is always with God; the response is with man. God will not violate our freedom of will. Since God does not need anything we can give—talent, money—obviously the one thing He desires is our will; we are free to give that.

He will introduce factors that affect our decision. It may be a dramatic factor, as in the Damascus road experience of Saul of Tarsus. It may be a stated condition, as in the case of the rich young ruler. These factors may be introduced by our prayers. My wife and I once prayed three years for a lost man. We were encouraged because we noticed obvious indications that the Holy Spirit was bringing him under an uncomfortable conviction. After three years, he finally accepted Christ, but today, in retrospect, the backward look at those years of prayer is a fascinating study in the interplay of the will of the Holy Spirit and his positive and negative reaction to it. He was free; God was free. Persistent prayer finally found the point at which he surrendered his life.

The fact that so many in the Bible rejected God or even rebelled against Him is proof that God did not force them into a decision. The fact that so many followed Him is proof that the will can cooperate with God. In any case, both the will of God and the will of human beings remain free. This gives glory to the drama of redemption.

For What Is It Proper to Pray?
The answer to this is stated without hesitation in Philippians 4:6—pray about everything. Nothing in the Bible encourages us to divide life into "secular" and "sacred" categories. Can you imagine Jesus having His earthly life categorized like that? It is foreign to the Jewish mentality, and the Christian writings nowhere approach any such division. However, there *is* the profane (not merely secular); the profane is actually anti-Christian. Christianity and Judaism alike hallow all of life as good. Jesus enjoyed eating. He blessed the wedding at Cana, and He enjoyed a variety of wholesome friendships. For Jesus, all of life was good.

There are some things, however, for which we should not ask. James 4:1-3 makes it clear that we are not to ask a thing in order to spend it solely on our pleasures. We are to pray for the will of God and the coming of His kingdom. Several years ago I attempted to make a survey of the answered prayers of the Bible. Among the various patterns I discovered was the fact that most of the answered prayers were concerned strictly with the advance of the divine work—such as Moses' prayers for the nation advancing through the desert. Fewer of the Bible prayers could be considered personal—such as Hannah's prayer for a son.

None of the personal prayers contradicted the nature and purposes of the divine work; in fact, they usually enhanced it. For example, Hannah's prayer produced Samuel, surely a pivotal figure in Israel's history (1 Sam. 1:10-20). Some time after my survey of the prayers of the Bible, I attempted to document the answered prayers over a specific time period in my own life and was amazed to discover the same proportions emerging—roughly seven-ninths of my own answered prayers were primarily concerned with the advance of the kingdom work of God, and two-ninths were personal—and yet all of the answered personal requests in some significant way accomplished a divine work that helped others and made a contribution to God's work in the church.

There are also inappropriate *ways* to pray, but these will be discussed in chapter 6.

Does God Hear the Prayers of Non-Christians?

This extremely knotty question will see different answers from different people, according to how they interpret the biblical information. Here, we must concern ourselves with the major, salient, unassailable facts as revealed in the Bible.

Fact 1. God loves all persons, wants them to come to Him, and will introduce factors into their lives to bring them to Himself. Naaman was a Syrian, a non-Jew, and probably never circumcised, and yet God answered his request for healing through Elisha. As a result, Naaman turned to Yahweh, the God of Israel; he confessed, "'Behold now, I know that there is no God in all the earth, but in Israel'" (2 Kings 5:15) and confessed that in the future he would serve only Yahweh (v. 17).

Fact 2. Jesus spoke tenderly of the love of God for the Gentiles when His own townspeople of Nazareth rejected Him. He referred specifically to God's feeding of the widow of Zarephath, in the Gentile region of Phoenicia, through Elijah, and to Naaman's healing. He healed the daughter of the Syrophoenician woman (Matt. 15:21-28).

Fact 3. God is free to use Christian, non-Christian, Jew, or Gentile in the accomplishing of His purposes, as He sees fit. He used the pagan rulers Nebuchadnezzar (Dan. 2—4), Darius (Dan. 6:4-27), and Cyrus (2 Chron. 36:22-23). All of these retained their paganism, and in none of these cases is there specific prayer, although Darius's beautiful decree (Dan. 6:26-27) comes very close. We must recognize, however, God's freedom to use whatever person or factor He wants to use. He even directed the speech of the pagan hireling Baalam (Num. 23:7-10,18-24).

Fact 4. Israel was given special instructions to love the alien and to include the stranger in their national life. Israel was told that God loves the alien and provides for him (Deut. 10:18-19). One section of the Levitical law provided that the alien in Israel should observe the law (Num. 15:15-29). Aliens could even elect to become Jews (Ex. 12:48; see also Deut. 23:8 and Gen. 17:27). The psalmist declared that the Lord protects the strangers (Ps. 146:9).

God's omniscience enables Him to hear all human discourse, holy and profane, and all these factors will interplay in accomplishing for a loving God those things His tenderness wants to accomplish as He hears desperate cries from the needy. He loves the widow, the poor, the stranger, and the orphan.

Fact 5. All life and all provision come from God. The psalmist declared, "The eyes of all look to Thee, and Thou dost give them their food in due time" (Ps. 145:15).

Fact 6. The Model Prayer demonstrates for us the fact that God always puts His business and His purposes ahead of all concerns any of us might have, whether we are Christian or non-Christian. An omnipresent, omnipotent, omniscient God is not too busy to attend to many things, but even God has priorities. The Christian has bases upon which to pray that other people do not have. Serious prayer, cooperating with God in the accomplishing of His purposes, is the prayer God wants most to hear and always gives priority to the bringing of His kingdom.

With all of these things in mind, we can conclude that God is sovereign. He is not limited by anything we believe about Him. Simply because He is God, He answers prayer according to His own wisdom.

The Christian is uniquely related to God as His child. There are many promises to answer prayer that God made solely to believers. This does not, however, limit God in His concern for all people.

Why Do Christians Pray in the Name of Jesus?

At least three different times in His last discourse, Jesus told us to offer our prayers in His name (John 14:13-14; 15:16; 16:23-24,26-27). He said that when His people were gathered in His name, He would be present (Matt. 18:20). His name is our legal authorization for prayer. He is our way to God (John 14:6); there is no other name under heaven by which we must be saved (Acts 4:12).

His name is now our name, "Christian," and the use of His name reflects our taking on His character; it is not a ritual. The seven sons of Sceva attempted to use Jesus' name outside His character, and the evil spirit they were exorcising overpowered them and wounded them (Acts 19:13-17). Jesus' name identifies our family; Paul addressed his first letter to the Corinthian church "to those . . . who in every place call upon the name of our Lord Jesus Christ" (1 Cor. 1:2).

His name appropriates all that God has done for us in Christ the Beloved. It is an acknowledgment that our highest, richest possession is in that identity. As the beggar pleaded for alms from Peter and John, Peter told him, "'I do not possess silver and gold, but what I do have I give to you: In the name of Jesus Christ the Nazarene—walk!'" (Acts 3:6).

His name appropriates all that is in the revealed character of God. It places us in the long line of those who have called upon the Lord's name through history. At the beginning of prayer history, after the birth of Enosh (man in his weakness), "then men began to call upon the name of the Lord" (Gen. 4:26). When Samuel was comforting Israel after their sin in demanding a king, he assured them, "'For the Lord will not abandon His people on account of His great name'" (1 Sam. 12:22).

The name of Jesus is the intensifying agent of unity in the body of Christ. I have seen the power of unity in Christ's name demonstrated many times. At Southwestern Seminary for many years one of my classes, for some inexplicable reason, has always seen a remarkable prayer bond develop early in the course. Although all my classes see remarkable answers to prayer, that class has seen a large number of unusual and dramatic answers—jobs found, marriages healed, the sick returned to health. I have not been able to determine why that course is so honored by the Lord, but its special blessing is demonstrated by the fact that graduates call back often to request prayer of that one class.

The use and honor of the name of Jesus were important to the New Testament churches. Thanksgiving in Ephesus was to be given in the name of Jesus (Eph. 5:20). Paul prayed that the name of Jesus might be glorified in the church at Thessalonica (2 Thess. 1:11-12). The use of Jesus' name is one indication of the centrality of Christ in New Testament times. The name of Yahweh had been important in the Old Testament since the giving of the third commandment (Ex. 20:7) and continued prominent in the later Old Testament writings (Deut. 28:58; Ps. 99:3). Jesus began the Model Prayer with the solemn phrase, "'Hallowed be Thy name.'" As revelation unfolded, the church legitimately attached to Jesus' name the traditional reverence it had always exhibited for the name of God. That reverence sprang from the biblical revelation itself and remains the basis on which we come to God and on which we offer our prayers.

Does God Always Answer Prayer?

Not all of the prayers in the Bible were answered—at least not always with a yes. No, of course, is an answer. Most of the unanswered prayers in Scripture (that is, the prayers which received a no answer) violate the principles of prayer in some significant way. Each of them is helpful in discerning the patterns and ways God works through prayer. As the Israelites once more rebelled in the wilderness, Moses petulantly asked to die (Num. 11:11-15). Moses used thirteen personal pronouns in this prayer; his eyes were off God and on himself. True prayer exalts God.

In Deuteronomy 3:23-29 Moses indicated that he had prayed to enter the Promised Land but that this was not to be allowed because in unbelief he had angrily struck the rock twice at Kadesh in disobedience to God's command to speak to the rock (Num. 20:8-12). On that occasion God answered Moses immediately that this would prevent him from entering the Promised Land; Moses referred to it in Deuteronomy 3:23-29; the final and merciful act in the drama came when God allowed him to survey the new land from the heights of Mount Nebo (Deut. 32:48-52). Some sin is irreversible. We ourselves establish consequences for our actions which God will not suspend.

King Saul's inquiry of the Lord about the Philistines camped at Shunem was not answered (1 Sam. 28:6). A long record of sin against David, against the nation, and against God had separated him from God. Isaiah later would write that the Lord's ear was not dull so that it could not hear, "but your iniquities have made a separation between you and your God" (Isa. 59:2). Interestingly enough, two chapters after Saul's inquiry, David's inquiry about pursuing the

Amalekites *was* answered (1 Sam. 30:8). This occurred in a time of great personal distress, when David had "strengthened himself in the Lord" (1 Sam. 30:6).

David's prayer for his son by Bathsheba to live was not answered (2 Sam. 12:15-20). David was praying for something about which God had already spoken. Nathan had warned him about his sin, " 'However, because by this deed you have given occasion to the enemies of the Lord to blaspheme, the child also that is born to you shall surely die' " (2 Sam. 12:14). This child was the fruit of lust. An answer to David's prayer would have become a continual reminder of his sin.

Elijah's prayer to die (1 Kings 19:4) is one of the strangest of the Bible prayers—not strange because God refused to answer, but strange that the faith of Elijah could be so shattered after his great victory at Carmel. God still had use for Elijah, and Elijah simply stepped out of the will of God in this prayer.

The prayer of Salome, James, and John that the two men sit at the right and left of Jesus was made from wrong motives (Matt. 20:20-21; praying from wrong motives will be discussed in the next chapter). Jesus pointed out a factor that still holds true today in many of our prayers: " 'You do not know what you are asking for' " (v. 22).

James and John also mistakenly asked that fire out of heaven consume the Samaritan village which refused to receive Christ (Luke 9:51-56). This seemingly normal reaction represents the mind of man, not the mind of Christ.

Jesus referred twice in His parables and once again in His teaching to types of unanswerable prayers. The parable of the rich man and Lazarus has the rich man in hades asking that his tongue be cooled and his brothers warned (Luke 16:19-31). This prayer was too late; it involved nothing that all true prayer in the Bible is—it involved no worship of God

(Ps. 141:2), and it exhibited no fellowship, no commonality with God. Another of Jesus' parables pictures a self-exalting Pharisee boasting of his righteousness (Luke 18:9-14). This is bragging, not praying. Again, it did not grow out of fellowship with God. In a similar vein, Jesus pointed out that the street-corner prayer of the hypocrites was not prayer (Matt. 6:5). It was unanswerable. His conclusion is rather chilling: "Truly I say to you, they have their reward in full."

All prayers are not answered with a yes, in part because so many of them are counter to the nature of God's laws and to the mind of Christ; then, too, some "prayer" is not really prayer. James 5:17 has a curious expression in the Greek; speaking of Elijah, James says, "In prayer he prayed." Halfheartedness and insincerity cannot characterize true prayer.

Not all unanswered prayer is a result of failure in our prayers. Sometimes unanswered prayer may derive from a test God is imposing. The recorded prayers of Job did not involve sin, and the test came, not because he was in sin, but because he was righteous. Tests are intended to prove both God's keeping power and our progress in His character.

Job's prayer to die (Job 6:8-9) was made in ignorance of the great heavenly council in Job 1 which was to be one of the great proofs of all time of the profound work that God can do in a man's life. Many of our prayers are in ignorance. There is no record of sin in any of Job's prayers. It is interesting that three of the most righteous men in the Bible—Moses, Elijah, and Job—all mistakenly prayed to die. It is also interesting that they received great boons from the Lord following their mistaken prayers.

We must be very careful about assuming that God is testing us or others when prayers are not answered. God deals with each of His children in the loving way that is best for their individual needs. The best we can do is to pray in trust and confidence.

We can often learn valuable lessons in trust and patience in times of difficulty and testing. Trials are not necessarily sent by God, but they can always be used by God to draw us closer to Him. Such times of difficulty often prepare us for God's best that is still awaiting us.

Does Prayer Change God's Mind?

After God rejected Saul from being king over Israel, Saul pleaded with Samuel to come with him so that he could worship the Lord once again. Samuel refused, for God's verdict was final. He told Saul, "'Also the Glory of Israel will not lie or change His mind; for He is not a man that He should change His mind'" (1 Sam. 15:29). Malachi quotes God as saying, "'I, the Lord, do not change; therefore you, O sons of Jacob, are not consumed'" (Mal. 3:6). The New Testament presents the same picture; God is the "Father of lights, with whom there is no variation, or shifting shadow" (Jas. 1:17).

We are often slow to discover the mind of God. God may have a specific end in view, with several possible routes toward that end. These various roads mean that the means of achieving God's end may be dynamic rather than static. God may now alter this or that road, may put up roadblocks, may redirect us in such a way that we who cannot see the end think that He seems to be changing. Our attention is on the road—and there are road rules—but God's attention is on the end. The attributes, purposes, and mind of God do not change, and we must be careful not to "read into" varying circumstances a purpose of God that would attribute change to Him.

What If Your Prayers Are Not Answered?

There are two main choices we may make—desist or

persist. Paul prayed three times that his "thorn in the flesh" be removed. For the sake of the kingdom, pride on the part of this great church planter would have been disastrous. To check that pride, the Lord denied Paul his request, saying, "'My grace is sufficient for you, for power is perfected in weakness'" (2 Cor. 12:9). Paul indicates that he desisted from praying this prayer after that, preferring to boast about his weaknesses in order to have the power of the indwelling Christ.

Daniel prayed in mourning for three weeks; the angel who came to encourage him told him,

> *Do not be afraid, Daniel, for from the first day that you set your heart on understanding this and on humbling yourself before your God, your words were heard, and I have come in response to your words (Dan. 10:12).*

The angel told him that he had been detained by a struggle with the "prince of the kingdom of Persia," but Michael had secured his release to come in answer to Daniel's prayer. At that point Daniel had been fasting and praying for three weeks; he persisted, and there resulted a mighty and terrifying vision.

These two mighty men of God were so in tune with God that they knew when to persist and when to desist. That is what frightens us today; few of us approach the keen spiritual sensitivity of a Paul or a Daniel. Nevertheless, the biblical record provides an example for us, and the potential of that kind of spiritual awareness is as great today as it was in the past.

We also must approach prayer with a willingness to accept God's actions with humility, regardless of our personal preferences. No doubt Zacharias and Elizabeth had long ago accepted a verdict of no when they prayed for a child, for they remained God's choice, even in their old age; they had not disqualified themselves with bitter resentment. Gabriel assured Zacharias, "'Do not be afraid, Zacharias, for your petition has been heard'" (Luke 1:13). This was a long delay, and yet "they were both righteous in the sight of God" (Luke 1:6). Their example is a live option for believers today who have not lost faith when answers seem long delayed.

Sometimes God Himself delays, as in the case of Zacharias; sometimes He allows evil forces to delay, as in Daniel's situation; sometimes the answer is no, as in the case of Paul. Those qualities most likely to suffer in our character today during a delay are: faith, patience, endurance, joy, and humble acceptance. We must guard against this loss, realizing that even delays can work out for our good.

When Is It Right to Pray for a Miracle?

Miracles in the Bible usually occurred in moments of desperation (Moses and the Israelites blocked at the Red Sea) or when all other hope of help had been exhausted (the various sick, lame, blind, or dumb who needed miracles of healing as they encountered Christ). Excepted from this are the miracles surrounding the death and resurrection of Christ, which are in a class by themselves. The latter served purposes different from the other biblical miracles.

The miracles had certain factors in common: (1) they brought glory to God; (2) they did not glorify man; (3) sometimes they validated the claims or the identity of God; and (4) they advanced the divine work significantly. There is a total absence of the capricious or the whimsical. There is an element of grandeur and awesome dignity about each of them. There is an element of (for lack of a better word) elegance about their execution. The latter is easily demonstrable in the miracles of Christ.

These same factors should exist today when we may expect a miracle. God may bring them together in our experience, and if He does, we may be sure He will enable us to recognize them and pray in faith that He finish what He obviously started.

Does God Hear One Person More than Another?

A man once approached me to pray for a situation in such a way that it became apparent that he was asking me to pray because he felt I might have more influence with God than he; maybe I could get God to do what he could not persuade Him to do. The Bible nowhere substantiates such a notion. This was how Saul was wanting to use Samuel (1 Sam. 15:24-25).

It is true, of course, that God can be pleased and displeased with us. He seeks spiritual worshipers; He "favors those who fear Him, those who wait for His lovingkindness" (Ps. 147:11). There is joy in heaven over one sinner who repents (Luke 15:7). We are told that the Lord takes pleasure in His people (Ps. 149:4).

Individuals may please Him. He asked Satan, "'Have you considered My servant Job? For there is no one like him on the earth, a blameless and upright man, fearing God and turning away from evil'" (Job 1:8). Enoch was "pleasing to God" (Heb. 11:5). The angel called Daniel a "man of high esteem" (Dan. 10:11,19). Jesus loved Martha, Mary, and Lazarus (John 11:5), and John calls himself the "disciple whom Jesus loved" (John 20:2). These examples could be multiplied; the point is that a human being can become pleasant to the Lord, a joy to Him.

Although the record indicates that these beloved of the Lord received unusual answers to prayer, their answers were not an indication of favoritism. Rather, they were obedient to the principles required by God and gave themselves with unstinting devotion to Him. They were not a *favorite* by arbitrary choice but were indeed *favored* because of the position they chose.

It is also evident that experienced prayer warriors can see factors, pray more intelligently, and weigh spiritual evidence in a way that prayerless people cannot. Many times I request prayer of certain people not because I think they "have influence with God" but because *I know they will pray*.

When the people of God become willing to exercise their privileges and prerogatives in prayer, great and mighty things will happen. His name will be glorified, and the world will become convinced that Jesus is indeed the Christ.

PERSONAL LEARNING ACTIVITY 10

A friend confides to you: "I've prayed and prayed, and it has done no good. I'm going to give up on prayer." What answer would you give to encourage your friend to

continue to pray? _____

_____

_____

Chapter 6

Hindrances

to Effective Prayer

Prayerlessness
Wrong Motives
Lack of Faith
Not Abiding
Rebellion and Sin
Lack of Importunity

James told us clearly, "You do not have because you do not ask" (Jas. 4:2). How strange that such a warning should have been necessary after so many injunctions to ask by Jesus Himself! Jesus told the woman at the well, " 'If you knew the gift of God, and who it is who says to you, "Give Me a drink," you would have asked Him, and He would have given you living water' " (John 4:10). This gentle offer was made to a woman who did not have the recorded promise that those who asked would receive. The numerous times Jesus used the word *ask* in His teaching are proof of the divine will to give. If progress in the Christian life depends on our prayers, if we are commanded to ask, if promises on a cosmic scale are made to those who ask—what would a waiting Father think if we refused to ask? The only possible conclusion would be that we are either not interested in spiritual progress or else that we intend to spurn the very Word of God.

Prayerlessness

There may be some who refuse to ask out of a hypocritical piety that refuses to believe God's promises. It is indeed true that we are not to test God (Deut. 6:16), but neither are we to spurn Him. The idolatrous king of Judah, Ahaz, attacked by the northern kingdom of Syria, was assured by the prophet Isaiah that he need only ask for a sign from

God. God would protect Judah, not for the sake of the faithless Ahaz but for the sake of God's people. Yet Ahaz assumed a superficially pious attitude: "'I will not ask, nor will I test the Lord!'"—a cloak for his determination to rely on an alliance with Assyria rather than Yahweh. Isaiah unmasked the hypocrisy: "'Is it too slight a thing for you to try the patience of men, that you will try the patience of my God as well?'" (Isa. 7:12-13).

God's promises, like His commands, are not optional. The Ahaz story is a graphic illustration of the fact that refusal to pray is an affront to a faithful God who has invited us to ask, seek, and knock. Prayerlessness is a statement to God that we do not believe that spiritual forces have the power to affect a world created by a spiritual being. We are agreeing with Ahaz that security is found in the visible, in the forces of this world, even though we are assured repeatedly that all creation is under His dominion (1 Chron. 29:11-12; Pss. 97:1; 103:19).

"'God is spirit'" (John 4:24), and it is He who ordained the way His world will function. There is a spiritual hand which never errs, a spiritual mind which always functions back of the functioning of this world. Pilate boasted of his own authority, but Jesus told him, "'You would have no authority over Me, unless it had been given you from above'" (John 19:11). Many men of great public or personal stature were forced to acknowledge that the Lord Himself is God—Nebuchadnezzar (Dan. 4:1-3); Darius (Dan. 6:25-27); Saul of Tarsus (Acts 9:1-16). It would be pointless to pray "for kings and all who are in authority" if we did not believe that our prayers actually affect thrones. Paul told Timothy that such prayers would secure a "tranquil and quiet life in all godliness and dignity" (1 Tim. 2:2).

There is only one kind of greatness taught in the Bible— spiritual greatness. Prayerfulness characterized the lives of Enoch, Abraham, Moses, Hannah, Samuel, David,

Hezekiah, Isaiah, Elijah, Elisha, Jeremiah, Daniel, Mary the mother of Jesus, Peter, Paul, John, and, above all, Jesus, to mention only a very few. Can you imagine Daniel or Abraham or Jesus functioning apart from prayer? A life filled with the Spirit cannot be empty of prayer.

Prayerlessness is sin. When Israel sinned against the Lord by demanding a king, Samuel assured them in their fear, "'Moreover, as for me, far be it from me that I should sin against the Lord by ceasing to pray for you'" (1 Sam. 12:23). Paul was not guilty of this sin; note how he prayed for his churches: "unceasingly" (Rom. 1:9); "always" (Phil. 1:4); and "night and day" (1 Thess. 3:10). He told Timothy, "I constantly remember you in my prayers night and day" (2 Tim. 1:3). Jesus' life was so prayerful that the disciples were moved to ask Him to teach them to pray (Luke 11:1). His prayer for the disciples is a model of intercession (John 17). Prayerlessness is never encountered in any of the great men or women of the Bible.

This one sin is the most serious of all the hindrances to prayer. It balks at the beginning—and no progress is made if we start wrong. Prayerlessness is deadly.

Wrong Motives
An attitude of selfishness resulting in wrong motives hinders effective prayer. James said, "You ask and do not receive, because you ask with wrong motives, so that you may spend it on your pleasures" (Jas. 4:3). When a person elevates his personal whims above those of others, the result is a separation, an isolation that loses sight of the larger goals of the body of Christ. Selfish desires pose one of the greatest dangers to personal growth and to the growth of the church.

Paul showed us that there is a legitimate prayer for self; his prayers for himself were for boldness to speak on behalf of the kingdom or to be able to travel to a church that needed him. Hannah prayed for a son, but she gave him to the Lord. The self in these cases is deeply involved with others; the mind of Christ is to be concerned primarily with the advance of the kingdom, the will of God, and the welfare of others. The self need not be selfish.

Selfishness poses a danger to the purposes God wants to accomplish. The psalmist wrote that the Israelites "craved intensely in the wilderness, and tempted God in the desert. So He gave them their request, but sent a wasting disease among them" (Ps. 106:14-15). In the rebellion at Taberah, "the rabble who were among them had greedy desires" (Num. 11:4); the psalmist said that they "put God to the test by asking food according to their desire" (Ps. 78:18). The provision of manna by Yahweh did not satisfy them; the psalmist goes on to say that this was both unbelief and distrust (Ps. 78:22). A selfish person will always be discontented.

The New Testament is even more specific. Paul, speaking of this rebellion, warned, "Now these things happened as examples for us, that we should not crave evil things, as they also craved" (1 Cor. 10:6). He wrote the church at Rome, "Make no provision for the flesh in regard to its lusts" (Rom. 13:14). He spelled out the principle in Galatians 5:17: "The flesh sets its desire against the Spirit, and the Spirit against the flesh; for these are in opposition to one another, so that you may not do the things that you please." Opposing natures cannot mix, and we must never mix opposing motives.

I have a "grand-dog," Penni, the dog that belongs to the family of my daughter. That dog has needs—food, water, and affection. I share those needs, but some of my needs are different from hers because our natures are different. My own pleasure in the music of Beethoven means nothing to her; she has no need in that area and no way of understanding my need. I can romp with her and run with her, but we can never listen to music together; she has no equipment to understand that part of my nature. Although we share certain things, she can partake of nothing uniquely human.

My animal needs are important, but they function best when they remain subservient to my spiritual needs. The animal part of me can serve the spirit, but I am most sublimely human when the spiritual is in control and dominates my entire being. This is why fasting can be a spiritual exercise. The animal needs are legitimate and healthy; they are not, in themselves, sin. The lesser, the animal, is subject to the greater, the spirit.

The spirit and the *body* are not in opposition, but when the *flesh* (not the body) becomes a principle, a control for the spirit, either through pride (Col. 2:28) or through lusts or any other manifestation (Gal. 5:19-21), we have lowered the standard of our high creation in Christ. Just as Penni cannot conceive or understand that which is peculiarly human, natural man cannot understand that which is peculiarly spirit (1 Cor. 2:14). And as the human is higher than the animal, the spiritual person lives in a higher dimension and understanding than the natural man. Jesus put it most succinctly: "'It is the Spirit who gives life; the flesh profits nothing'" (John 6:63).

This is not to say that everyday human needs are not important. The Father knows that we need the ordinary things of life, and He is concerned about providing them for us (Matt. 6:32). The point is that we are to give priority to His kingdom as we trust Him to supply our needs (Matt. 6:33).

Selfishness brings into our experience a danger so great that God knows He cannot coddle us with answers hostile to the very thing He is working to achieve in us. I would not give a murderer a knife to pamper one of his whims. God will not risk putting into our hands a hazard in order to satisfy an unhealthy desire. Prayers offered from totally selfish and wrong motives cannot be answered.

Lack of Faith

Faith is the basis of any genuine relationship; the more sensitive and dynamic a relationship is, the greater the faith that must enter into it. The writer of Hebrews stated unequivocally, "Without faith it is impossible to please Him, for he who comes to God must believe that He is, and that He is a rewarder of those who seek Him" (Heb. 11:6). Failure to believe means that we think God is a liar, that He is mocking us. No relationship is possible if there is no faith.

Wavering is the opposite of God's character. He does not change. One of the secrets of successful praying is to duplicate God's character. James puts a special emphasis on this matter of character where prayer is concerned:

> *If any of you lacks wisdom, let him ask of God, who gives to all men generously and without reproach, and it will be given to him. But let him ask in faith without any doubting, for the one who doubts is like the surf of the sea driven and tossed by the wind. For let not that man expect that he will receive anything from the Lord, being a double-minded man, unstable in all his ways (Jas. 1:5-8).*

In the world, normally you earn what you get. But in God's kingdom, you get what you believe. After giving the figure of speech about faith moving mountains, Jesus said, "'Therefore I say to you, all things for which you pray and ask, believe that you have received them, and they shall be granted you'" (Mark 11:24). The believing is the receiving, and without the believing there is no receiving.

Faith is the cup we offer to God to fill, and it is a

measuring cup. When the centurion demonstrated great faith, Jesus told him, "'Let it be done to you as you have believed'" (Matt. 8:13). Apparently the centurion's faith was equal to the situation, for His servant was healed "that very hour." As the officer demonstrated such faith that he believed that Jesus could heal across distances, Jesus marveled, "'Truly I say to you, I have not found such great faith with anyone in Israel'" (v. 10).

He often measured the faith of those who came to Him. He asked two blind men seeking healing, "'Do you believe that I am able to do this?'" Upon their yes answer, he told them, "'Be it done to you according to your faith'" (Matt. 9:29). Their faith, too, measured high, for their eyes were opened.

Two causes may underlie the difficulty some people have in believing. One would be a fear that God does not want to give. The repeated invitations to ask are surely proof of the divine intention. Jesus demonstrated His own desire that we believe on the occasion of the raising of Lazarus. As He stood before the open tomb, He prayed: "'Father, I thank Thee that Thou heardest Me. And I knew that Thou hearest Me always; but because of the people standing around I said it, that they may believe that Thou didst send Me'" (John 11:41-42). This is the desire of God Himself—*that we may believe*.

The second cause is a fear that the thing we are asking is too great or too difficult. The irrationality of this fear is unmasked when we recognize that this is actually a fear that God cannot perform. The word of the Lord to Jeremiah was, "'Behold, I am the Lord, the God of all flesh; is anything too difficult for Me?'" (Jer. 32:27). At the foot of the Mount of Transfiguration, when the pleading father asked Jesus if He could do anything for his demon-possessed son, Jesus exclaimed, "'If You can! All things are possible to him who believes'" (Mark 9:23). God is the possessor of all riches; we never need wonder if He can afford what we might ask. He is the author of all capabilities; we never need wonder if He can produce.

Faith changes behavior. The Greek word for *receiving* and *taking* is the same. Jesus said that if we asked we would receive; if we ask, we are to take. Paul's behavior grew out of his prayer. From prison he wrote the Philippians, "I know that this shall turn out for my deliverance through your prayers and the provision of the Spirit of Jesus Christ" (Phil. 1:19). No worry, no apprehension pervades the rest of this letter; this is, in fact, the most joy-filled letter in the New Testament.

The work, after all, is not dependent on our resources, talents, or training. It is Christ who is in us (Gal. 2:20), who wants us to believe, through whom we have access to God (Eph. 3:12). "Faith comes from hearing, and hearing by the word of Christ" (Rom. 10:17). Serious attendance on the right word is the secret to faith. That word has been given.

If we believe God, we can leave the case in His hands. Paul wrote that we are to "be anxious for nothing" (Phil. 4:6) and then assured us that the peace of God would "guard your hearts and your minds in Christ Jesus" (v. 7). Faith frees us to do the work of God without impediment from within.

The function of faith is not simply to get something done. Faith is the basis of our relationship with God. That relationship is significant truth—the truth of a divinely initiated relationship to a great Father, a caring Shepherd, and a gentle Master. We can put our confidence in such a gracious Lord.

Not Abiding
Failure to maintain a vital relationship with God hinders prayer. Any relationship must be maintained, and the most important relationship in life is especially sensitive. Jesus

told the disciples, " 'If you abide in Me, and My words abide in you, ask whatever you wish, and it shall be done for you' " (John 15:7). Anyone can make a superficial claim of any cause; the world and the kingdom see many "flashes in the pan." Proof of genuineness is enduring in our profession.

Less than this is not truly genuine. Paul wrote that God would "render to every man according to his deeds: to those who by perseverance in doing good seek for glory and honor and immortality, eternal life" (Rom. 2:6-7). Each of these words is cosmic in scope—glory, honor, immortality, eternal life. How long did it take David to win glory? Or Daniel to establish honor? There is nothing temporary in the work of Joseph, Samuel, Paul, or Jesus. Love "bears all things, believes all things, hopes all things, endures all things" (1 Cor. 13:7). Abiding is not accomplished in an afternoon's time. This is not to say that only the spiritually mature can pray effectively. Nor is it to advocate spiritual elitism. God hears the prayers of all His children. It is to say, however, that a continuing relationship with Christ enhances prayer.

The word *walk* is an important word in the New Testament. It is a picture word, describing what it means to abide in Christ. It describes the continuing daily life of the Christian. John revealed that that continuing process is proof of our belonging to Christ: "By this we know that we are in Him: the one who says he abides in Him ought himself to walk in the same manner as He walked" (1 John 2:5-6). Paul was fond of the word *walk;* he advised the Ephesians to walk in love, to walk as light, and to walk wisely (Eph. 5:2,8,15). If it is Christ we are abiding in, we cannot comfortably walk any other way.

God is more interested in a good root system than He is in the foliage of our lives. We tend to dress up the foliage, but God wants a healthy, extensive root system. He concluded the parable of the sower by observing that the "'seed in the good ground, these are the ones who have heard the word in an honest and good heart, and hold it fast, and bear fruit with perseverance'" (Luke 8:15).

On my first sabbatic leave, my family lived in Spain. It was a fascinating year of observing the extensive farming of grapes. On many of the farms, the grapes are not slender vines, as so often seen in America, but have thick trunks. We were astonished at the end of the harvest to see the Spaniards cutting down those tree-like vines! But the next season their stumps began to put out shoots that indicated that they were not dead. Most surprising of all was to watch the workers prune the branches so thoroughly. Once we even saw a farmer placing rocks on the stumps to force the shoots to grow exactly as he wanted. It was evident that the root systems were undamaged; the life of the plant depends only a little on its foliage but very much on its roots. To the Spanish farmers, foliage was secondary. It was fruit that was important, and two workers entered into the process of getting that fruit—maintaining good roots and pruning the branches.

Why is abiding important? It is one aspect of endurance. It is proof of faithfulness. Only in abiding is importunity a real option. It is a demonstration of a part of our character that is like God, whose righteousness endures forever (Ps. 111:3) and whose name is everlasting (Ps. 135:13).

Abiding will entail much time, much prayer, much attention to the biblical directives, and much cleaving to the Lord. For me, at least, it has involved a serious attempt to memorize much Scripture. Most encouraging of all is the fact that abiding requires no talent or training; it requires only perseverance.

Rebellion and Sin

The Scriptures emphatically claim that an attitude of

rebellion in the heart or sin in the life hinders effective prayer. The psalmist said, "If I regard wickedness in my heart, the Lord will not hear" (Ps. 66:18). An ancient indictment of Israel has been a solemn warning throughout time:

> *Behold, the Lord's hand is not so short that it cannot*
> *save; neither is His ear so dull that it cannot hear.*
> *But your iniquities have made a separation between*
> *you and your God, and your sins have hidden His*
> *face from you, so that He does not hear (Isa. 59:1-2)*

Any sin will annul the authority of our prayers, but the Bible specifically names several sins—besides those others discussed in this chapter—that place an immediate block on our prayers. The first of these is a deliberate shutting of our ears against need. "He who shuts his ear to the cry of the poor will also cry himself and not be answered" (Prov. 21:13). Indifference to need is out of the character of God and foreign to the spirit of prayer.

Ezekiel quoted God as saying: "'Son of man, these men [elders of Israel] have set up their idols in their hearts, and have put right before their faces the stumbling block of their iniquity. Should I be consulted by them at all?'" (Ezek. 14:3). God will not be consulted by anyone who has elevated something in the heart above Himself. Note that the warning is not against idols on the altar—it is against idols in the heart. Sometimes we can put noble and worthy things, good in themselves, above God. God will brook nothing placed above Himself.

The sin of hypocrisy in prayer reaps its own reward, but it reaps nothing from the Lord (Matt. 6:5; Mark 12:40). Pretense in prayer is speaking to human beings rather than God. When one prays for the sake of appearance, he gets what appearance can give. Fleshly prayer will bear no spiritual fruit.

Paul warned against anger in prayer: "Therefore I want the men in every place to pray, lifting up holy hands, without wrath and dissension" (1 Tim. 2:8). Again, anger is not duplicating the character of God. It is true that anger is an attribute of God, but His anger is different from the anger of people. God never "gets mad." The anger of God is a permanent, unchanging attribute of His holy nature. He is eternally angry at sin, unrighteousness, and injustice, attributes opposite His character. His anger never smolders or flares; it is, like His purity, transcendent, other, holy. On the other hand, "the anger of man does not achieve the righteousness of God" (Jas. 1:20). Expressing the character of God is the biblical norm for a new person in Christ. That character may fail to be expressed in daily life; it *must* be expressed in prayer, if the prayer is truly prayer.

Being in conflict and wrong relationship with others hinders effective prayer. Jesus Himself gave us the strongest warnings against offering out of a bitter heart maintaining a broken relationship:

> *If therefore you are presenting your offering at the altar, and there remember that your brother has something against you, leave your offering there before the altar, and go your way; first be reconciled to your brother, and then come and present your offering (Matt. 5:23-24).*

This warning applies primarily to our need of forgiveness from others. Our offenses usually grow out of selfish expressions—the antithesis of our character as children of God. It is an expression of humility, of great value in the kingdom, to seek forgiveness.

Equally, we must be willing to forgive others. Jesus' word is plain—" 'If you forgive men for their transgressions, your heavenly Father will also forgive you. But if you do not forgive men, then your Father will not forgive your transgressions'" (Matt. 6:14-15). It is Godlike to forgive.

An especially important relationship for accomplishing great things through prayer is that of marriage. Peter advised, "You husbands likewise, live with your wives in an understanding way, as with a weaker vessel, since she is a woman; and grant her honor as a fellow-heir of the grace of life, so that your prayers may not be hindered" (1 Pet. 3:7). The bond of marriage is strong in Scripture, but the relationship is fragile and must be handled sensitively, in love and understanding. Difficulties in that relationship can have an adverse effect on the prayer life.

Outer conflict is a sign of inner conflict, and conflict is foreign to the nature of the kingdom of God. We are told, "If possible, so far as it depends on you, be at peace with all men" (Rom. 12:18). There is a suggestion here that at times one person or party may be innocent and yet have to deal with a second party unwilling to make peace. Our main responsibility is for that part which depends on us. Again, Paul exhorted, "Let us pursue the things which make for peace and the building up of one another" (Rom. 14:19). *That* we can do. The importance of this pursuit is seen in the number of times it is enjoined in Scripture (Ps. 34:14; 2 Tim. 2:22; Heb. 12:14). The life of Christ in the individual and in the larger body should be a whole life, a unified life, integrated and without conflict. Splintering what God unites interferes with the other work of God—His work through our prayers.

Lack of Importunity

It was Jesus who, from His teaching, valued persistence most highly (see chapter 2, especially on Luke 11:5-13; 18:1-8). God works in process, always perfect in its timing, but sometimes discouraging to us if faith is not strong.

Mark 4:26-29 describes the imperceptible growth of a seed to its ultimate harvest and assumes the patience of the farmer as a part of his understanding of the meaning of process.

Importunity accomplishes much in our growth. It toughens faith. It establishes the reality of abiding and endurance. It proves earnestness, humility, obedience, and patience. We are to be slow to anger but also slow to give up.

Even from a human standpoint, it is easy to see the reasonableness and the need for persistence. Again and again, a friend will plead with me, "T. W., please don't stop praying for me." When the Philistines mustered against Israel at Mizpah, the Israelites begged Samuel, "'Do not cease to cry to the Lord our God for us, that He may save us from the hand of the Philistines'" (1 Sam. 7:8). Paul asked the Ephesian church to "be on the alert with all perseverance and petition for all the saints, and pray on my behalf" (Eph. 6:18-19). It encourages anyone to know that he or she is being prayed for—and that is one reason why it may be pleasing to God.

Several sins are named as particular hindrances to prayer, but any sin efficiently blocks the action of prayer. The hindrance is from our side. In sin, we are unlike God, and we cannot understand Him. In sin, we are blinded and do not know what to ask for. In sin, we act apart from His nature, and this brings blocks from God in our paths, which, if we are sensitive, will suggest better ways. Not receiving answers, many become bitter and even more estranged from God. Sin begets sin (Jas. 3:16) and confuses our prayer life.

Sometimes, a part of the delay we experience in prayer is the responsibility of divine wisdom. God cannot perpetuate error or unholiness. If He did that, the answer to prayer would itself be sin, and God cannot sin. He will not allow blindness to worsen with an improper answer or character to soften with too soon an answer. If we sin, He will lovingly bring us back to a point where we can begin learning again of His grand and perfect plan for our lives. That plan will be finished, and the body of Christ will be established through our prayers. That is His method.

PERSONAL LEARNING ACTIVITY 11
Match the following passages of Scripture concerning prayer with the references in the Bible.

___1. "'Moreover, as for me, far be it from me that I should sin against the Lord by ceasing to pray for you.'"

a. Hebrews 11:6

___2. "I constantly remember you in my prayers night and day."

b. James 1:5

___3. "Without faith it is impossible to please Him, for he who comes to God must believe that He is, and that He is a rewarder of those who seek Him."

c. 1 Samuel 12:23

___4. "If any of you lacks wisdom, let him ask of God."

d. John 15:7

___5. "'Be it done to you according to your faith.'"

e. Jeremiah 32:27

___6. "'Behold, I am the Lord, the God of all flesh; is anything too difficult for me?'"

f. 2 Timothy 1:3

___7. "'If you abide in Me, and My words abide in you, ask whatever you wish, and it shall be done for you.'"

g. Matthew 9:29

Answers: 1. c, 2. f, 3. a, 4. b, 5. g, 6. e, 7. d

Chapter 7

Prayer in the

Church—Then and Now

If we examine the expansion of the church in the Book of Acts and look at its prayers as recorded in Acts and the Epistles, we see convincing proof of the power of prayer. The early church had innumerable obstacles—Christianity was unknown, and it was opposed by the authorities wherever it spread, it suffered constantly from false accusations and rumors, and it tended to attract the lower classes. Yet by the end of the first century, it had spread in exactly the geographical pattern commissioned by Jesus—Jerusalem, Judea, Samaria, and the "uttermost part of the earth," points in Europe and Asia Minor far distant from its seedbed.

The expansion was such that it paved the way for an entirely new pattern of divine work, hardly conceivable in Judaism. This rapid geographical and idealogical shift could have been accomplished only by supernatural forces. The instrument of expansion was the church, and the force the church was using was prayer. Paul was one of the primary tools, but thousands of Christians scattered by the persecution also were used. These became firebrands to ignite the fire of the divine heat all over the Mediterranean world. Many of those firebrands had learned the divine method in Jerusalem, where prayer saturated the work of that first Christian church.

Prayer—an Important Part of the Life of the Earliest Church

The birth of the church occurred in an atmosphere of prayer and praise. After the ascension, the disciples "returned to Jerusalem with great joy, and were continually in the temple, praising God" (Luke 24:52-53). This evidently was not private prayer, and it provided the climate for an ongoing community life-style of praying together. Much of that prayer was probably prayer for the guidance of the Lord.

The Old Testament precedent was to look to God for guidance. It was an important part of Jewish history; the psalmist often sang of the divine leadership (Pss. 23:2-3; 31:3). Ezra saw the guiding hand of God in the supplying of the "man of insight" when his expedition back to Jerusalem needed Levites: "According to the good hand of our God upon us they brought us a man of insight" (Ezra 8:18), as well as enough Levites to function in the temple services. Many songs sang of God's guidance toward Canaan. The song of the Levites after the new celebration of the Feast of Tabernacles upon their return to Jerusalem from captivity acknowledged that their guidance was from ancient days: "The pillar of cloud did not leave them by day, to guide them on their way, nor the pillar of fire by night, to light for them the way in which they were to go" (Neh. 9:19).

The guidance of the Holy Spirit. Zacharias' prophecy had said that the coming Messiah would "guide our feet into the way of peace" (Luke 1:79). Jesus had promised that the Holy Spirit would guide into all truth (John 16:13). God would guide the church, as He had always guided Israel. In this bracing atmosphere of buoyant expectation, the church prayed for guidance in the selection of a replacement for Judas among the twelve: " 'Thou, Lord, who knowest the hearts of all men, show which one of these two [Joseph or Matthias] Thou hast chosen' " (Acts 1:24).

Guidance was important to the infant church. It did not yet have the New Testament Scriptures for help and instruction. Ahead of it lay expansion on a scale unimaginable at that time, miracles, persecution, separation, and scattering. Unaware of the proportions of the monumental task ahead of it, the church turned to prayer, guided by the experience of the history of Israel, its spiritual instincts, and, above all, the Holy Spirit Himself. He had been promised in the last discourse; they had been commanded to wait on His empowering (Luke 24:49); and the final word of Christ before He ascended was that they would receive power when He came upon them (Acts 1:8).

From the events in Acts 2 onward, God's guidance was specifically the guidance of the Holy Spirit. The entire apostolic record indicates that the church looked to Him as guide, prayed with His specific guidance in mind, and credited Him with being the fullness of God working in them. He became the instrument of spiritual birth and spiritual work; He protected the church in danger; and He initiated the great missionary expansion of the church.

The life of the church in prayer. Repeatedly Luke records the early church as being of one mind or of one heart (Acts 1:14; 2:46; 4:32). This unity is the basis of Paul's appeal to the Corinthian church to understand the interworking of the parts of the body (1 Cor. 12—14). He told them, "If one member suffers, all the members suffer with it; if one member is honored, all the members rejoice with it" (1 Cor. 12:26). The church was an organism, with interdependent parts that needed one another to function properly. Later Paul would entreat another church to be "diligent to preserve the unity of the Spirit in the bond of peace" (Eph. 4:3).

This bond secures awesome authority with God. Jesus had promised: "'If two of you agree on earth about anything that they may ask, it shall be done for them by My

Father who is in heaven. For where two or three have gathered together in My name, there I am in their midst'" (Matt. 18:19-20). The believer is the temple of the Holy Spirit (1 Cor. 6:19). When two of these temples filled with the Holy Spirit gather, a new and even more powerful expression of the presence of Christ Himself works outward with fearsome energy.

As the disciples awaited the promise of the Spirit after Christ's ascension, "these all with one mind were continually devoting themselves to prayer, along with the women, and Mary the mother of Jesus, and with His brothers" (Acts 1:14). *That* was the atmosphere that prepared the way for Pentecost! After Pentecost brought the first great ingathering, that same atmosphere continued: "They were continually devoting themselves to the apostles' teaching and to fellowship, to the breaking of bread and to prayer" (Acts 2:42). Small wonder that "everyone kept feeling a sense of awe; and many wonders and signs were taking place through the apostles" (Acts 2:43)!

Isaiah's ancient epithet of the temple as a "house of prayer" was being fully realized in the new household of God. Paul called this new body the "temple of God," where God's own Spirit dwelt (1 Cor. 3:16; the pronoun in this verse is plural). The life of this body was mediated through prayer, and the dominant spirit of that continuing prayer was praise (Acts 2:47).

The fact that prayer was the central activity of the apostles is shown by the resolution of the conflict in Acts 6. The seven men selected to distribute food were chosen so that the apostles could devote themselves to prayer and the ministry of the word (Acts 6:4). After the men were chosen, they were set aside by prayer (Acts 6:6).

When Paul and his party arrived in Philippi, they began their work by looking for "a place of prayer," and it was there, in the place of prayer, that the first European church was born (Acts 16:13-15). Later, the Philippian jailer was converted as God worked through the midnight prayers of Paul and Silas (Acts 16:25-33). The churches of the first century did not need to debate the importance of prayer; they turned to prayer naturally, instinctively. Wherever Christianity found a nesting place, that place rapidly became a "place of prayer," and the presence of Christ, through the power of the Holy Spirit, began working outward from the assembled body of new believers.

Prayer protected the church in crisis. Soon after the inception of the new body, danger confronted its members. Peter and John had been the instrument for the healing of a crippled beggar at the gate of the Temple; the reaction provided Peter with an opportunity for a convincing sermon, whereupon he and John were arrested. They then presented an unanswerable argument to the Sanhedrin, and the Sanhedrin, helpless to dispute the sermon and the events, released the two men but warned them not to teach or speak in Jesus' name. The church immediately went to prayer and asked eloquently for boldness of speech. "When they had prayed, the place where they had gathered together was shaken, and they were all filled with the Holy Spirit, and began to speak the word of God with boldness" (Acts 4:31).

Ever after that, continuing danger was an invitation to continuing prayer. Herod Agrippa I discovered that persecuting the church pleased the Jewish leaders, and so he proceeded to execute James, the brother of John, and to imprison Peter. The church prayed fervently, and Peter was miraculously delivered (Acts 12:5-11).

Danger and hazard would be an ever-present accompaniment to the spread of the church and to its work after that. The letter of the Jerusalem church to the church at Antioch to resolve the question over circumcision described its bearers, Paul, Barnabas, Judas called Barsabbas, and Silas, as "men who have risked their lives for the name of our Lord Jesus Christ" (Acts 15:26). Paul wrote the Corinthians that he was "in danger every hour" (1 Cor. 15:30) and later described to them a wide variety of dangers and circumstances he endured—imprisonment, lashing, beating, stoning, shipwreck, near drowning, betrayal (2 Cor. 11:23-26). Persecution hounded the early Christians on every hand, and they quickly found that the one reliable resource they could revert to was prayer.

Through prayer, blessing and fruit resulted from the very factors that threatened the church. Imprisoned at Philippi, Paul and Silas "were praying and singing hymns of praise to God" (Acts 16:25), and the miraculous earthquake that followed enabled Paul to speak that word which brought the jailer to Christ. The participants in that continuing first-century drama knew that they could not have survived without prayer nor could they have propagated the faith without prayer.

PERSONAL LEARNING ACTIVITY 12

Read 2 Corinthians 11:23-26. In these verses Paul wrote of his sufferings and trials as a Christian. List as many of the difficulties he faced as you can find in the verses.

_____	_____	_____
_____	_____	_____
_____	_____	_____
_____	_____	_____

Prayer and the birth of missions. In prayer, as in salvation, the initiative is with God. It is God who leads,

God who opens. There is a clear indication that the missionary movement was initiated first in the hearts of the missionaries to be sent, then in the church that was to send them. It began in Antioch, where a mighty group of prophets and teachers was assembled. "While they were ministering to the Lord and fasting, the Holy Spirit said, 'Set apart for Me Barnabas and Saul for the work to which I have called them'" (Acts 13:2). This seems to indicate that Barnabas and Saul already knew; they had been called. Now the Holy Spirit called the church to send them.

Sending in an appropriate manner is as important as hearing the call, and they were sent with prayer. "Then, when they had fasted and prayed and laid their hands on them, they sent them away" (Acts 13:3). The next verse could aptly describe the expansion of the church as seen in the rest of the Book of Acts: "Being sent out by the Holy Spirit." Imagine tackling the job of exporting a new faith, born in Judaism, outside the borders of Israel without prayer! The Holy Spirit initiated the missions movement in prayer, communicated to all the participants in prayer, and carried out what He had instigated through their prayers.

Prayer continued to be an important factor in the ongoing mission of the church. On the return part of their first missionary journey, Paul and Barnabas revisited churches they had established: "When they had appointed elders for them in every church, having prayed with fasting, they commended them to the Lord in whom they had believed" (Acts 14:23). Prayer contributed greatly to the founding of the Philippian church (Acts 16:16,25). When Paul met with the Ephesian elders at Miletus, "he knelt down and prayed with them all" (Acts 20:36). As he left Tyre, the entire congregation accompanied him to the ship. "After kneeling down on the beach and praying, we said farewell to one another" (Acts 21:5).

Most conclusive of all, however, are the numerous

teachings on prayer in the Epistles, the recorded prayers of Paul, and the requests made by him for the prayers of the churches. The abundant references to prayer in the letters of Paul sprinkle in chronologically throughout his journeys as he planted churches in Asia Minor and Europe. Prayer was the life of the church, its breath. The spiritual work was done with spiritual resources.

Prayer—an Important Part of Church Life Today
When Paul wrote Timothy a set of instructions to help him pastor the church at Ephesus, he incidentally left us some valuable information on public worship. He told Timothy:

> *First of all, then, I urge that entreaties and prayers, petitions and thanksgivings, be made on behalf of all men, for kings and all who are in authority, in order that we may lead a tranquil and quiet life in all godliness and dignity (1 Tim. 2:1-2).*

This is written for the practice of the church. Later he would enjoin public prayer again (v. 8).

Even if the early church had not followed the Hebrew pattern of worship, the psalms would have remained important throughout Christian history. Hymns and spiritual songs played a major part (Eph. 5:19; Col. 3:16) and were, of course, closely related to prayer. The pattern of dependence on prayer as the foundation of and basis for safety, fellowship in the unity of the Spirit, and expansion of the body has remained. Public prayer should always be a vital part of the worship of the church.

Intercessory prayer especially must be a regular activity of the church. The plea to the Roman church for their prayers for Paul is addressed to them in the plural—the entire church was being asked to pray for him (Rom. 15:30). He made similar requests to the Ephesians (Eph. 6:19), to the Thessalonians (1 Thess. 5:25), and to other churches. No doubt there was much private and small-group prayer also; that would have been consistent with the atmosphere of the time. Paul's own prayers brighten the pages of his letters.

The church family should also pray for guidance in its ongoing ministry. If Christ is the head (Eph. 5:23), we must look to Him. He expects His sheep to recognize His voice and follow Him:

> *He who enters by the door is a shepherd of the sheep. To him the doorkeeper opens, and the sheep hear his voice, and he calls his own sheep by name, and leads them out. When he puts forth all his own, he goes before them, and the sheep follow him because they know his voice (John 10:2-4).*

What we are to pray for in that ongoing ministry is well documented in Paul's prayers for the churches (Col. 1:9-12; Eph. 3:14-19; see chap. 4 for more on these).

The church should pray for the work of Christ everywhere. The universality of the churches' concern is shown in their wide sharing with one another, sometimes across considerable geographical distance. The church at Syrian Antioch shared with the Judean Christians (Acts 11:29). Paul directed the Corinthians to make a "collection for the saints" in Jerusalem (1 Cor. 16:1-3). He told them that the Macedonians shared generously of their means (2 Cor. 8:1-5).

Not only were they to share in needs, but they were to participate by means of prayer in the work of all the saints. The word *all* pervades the injunction to the Ephesians to pray—"With all prayer and petition pray at all times in the Spirit, and . . . be on the alert with all perseverance and petition for all the saints" (Eph. 6:18). Provincialism could not dominate the thinking of this new people of God, as it had in Judaism. Their world was as big as the one God had placed them in.

PERSONAL LEARNING ACTIVITY 13

Make a prayer list for the needs of your church. Commit yourself to pray daily for the needs and persons listed below.

1. *Church Leaders*   2. *Church Programs*

_____   _____

_____   _____

3. *World Missions*

_____

_____

Prayer—an Important Part of Home Life

The title of God which Jesus gave us to use in our prayers suggests something of His view of the home and its role. Paul was later to call the body of believers the "household of faith" (Gal. 6:10) and "God's household" (Eph. 2:19). That figure of speech and the name "Father" for the first person of the Trinity originated in an ideal familiar to Judaism—a family with strong, loving, caring parents and children who were loyal and representative of parental training.

Homes and households were important in the Gospels. The devout household of Zacharias and Elizabeth (Luke 1:6) provided the environment for the shaping of John the Baptist. The home of Zebedee, Salome, James, and John furnished Christ Himself with love and with followers. When Andrew perceived the identity of Christ, "he found first his own brother Simon, and said to him, 'We have found the Messiah'" (John 1:41). Jesus found refuge in the home of Mary, Martha, and Lazarus. Since He visited their home often, it must have refreshed Him, and John recorded that He loved them deeply (John 11:5).

Conversion to Christianity often took place by family blocks. Jesus told Zaccheus, "'Today salvation has come to this house'" (Luke 19:9). A plural number was baptized in the remarkable conversion account of Cornelius (Acts 10:47-48). The entire household of the Philippian jailer came to the Lord at one time (Acts 16:33). Family households often became the meeting place of a local church (Rom. 16:5; Philem. 2).

It was natural that the Christian community adopt the Jewish standard for homes. The strength of the home provided Jesus with a figure of speech to indicate the incongruity of a divided family remaining strong. He was actually stating His own unity with the Spirit of God and, by implication, the strength of a unified household (Matt. 12:25). Married couples were to demonstrate solidarity and unity of purpose, especially in their prayers. Peter's command for husbands to live considerately with their wives implied an understanding that their unified prayers would accomplish much. This prayer force must not be impeded (1 Pet. 3:7).

I am one who can speak of a lifetime of knowing the "family altar." My parents established the pattern of family devotions before I was born. Every evening as I grew up we would gather in the living room, talk about our day, read the Bible together, and offer a prayer. I can still vividly remember my parents thanking the Lord nightly for their two boys and asking His guidance in this or that matter as they trained us for kingdom service. Prayer came naturally to my brother and me because we never knew life apart from it. It would require many pages to recount moving incidents we experienced over the years in that daily altartime, some amusing, some poignant, but all pointing to the centrality of the reign of Christ in our home. It provided us with a security that has never been shaken and a faith in the reality of divine provision and protection in all circumstances.

Partly through the influence of that background, my wife and I established the practice of family devotions together more than a year before we married. That, in turn, led to other family traditions—a family psalm, a family hymn, annual home Thanksgiving services, and many lovely moments through all of our years that deepened the roots established by my parents many years ago. My wife's cancer and chemotherapy saw new and convincing proofs of the power of a strong married bond validating the promise of Scripture. *The stronger the bond, the more powerful and efficacious the prayer*! As far back as my daughter and my grandchildren will ever remember, home was a happy, praying place, a strong refuge with Christ at the center, Christ made manifest by prayer.

The home and the church today have more control over the course of this world than any civic authority or power. Any spiritual prayer in Jesus' name carries tremendous authority; in the unified prayer of Christians together that authority wields unimaginable power. The work of God and the advance of the kingdom are in the hands of the church.

Chapter 8

Developing

an Effective Prayer Life

Prayer, and for that matter, all our thought life, needs a shape—the shape of the mind of Christ. The most effective tool we have for shaping our thoughts are the thoughts of God as they are revealed in the Bible. The psalmist was delighted with them; he sang, "The words of the Lord are pure words; as silver tried in a furnace on the earth, refined seven times" (Ps. 12:6). Regular reading of the Bible is a way of exposing our mind to God's thoughts. The more exposure we give our minds to the Bible, provided it is interpreted according to Christ's example and teaching, the more likely we are to be conformed to the pattern of Christ's character.

Prayer—a Companion Discipline to Bible Study

Years ago I had reached a point in my devotions where I gave large blocks of time to prayer and only a few minutes each morning to Bible study. Then I heard "Preacher" E. F. Hallock, well known for his teaching on prayer, speak in the chapel of Southwestern Baptist Theological Seminary. "Preacher" Hallock made the statement that we should not have to choose between time in the Bible and time in prayer but that if a choice had to be made, it would be more important that God speak to the individual than that a person speak to God. That statement reformed my prayer life, not only in the amount of time I allotted in my personal devotions to studying and meditating on Scripture, but in the very tenor of my prayers, as I found myself increasingly being shaped by the words of Scripture lodged in my subconscious.

Scripture quickens its hearers. It enlivens our desire for the things of God and satisfies that yearning for God that is natural to the Christian. When Jesus explained Scripture to Cleopas and his companion on the road to Emmaus, they exclaimed to one another, "'Were not our hearts burning within us while He was speaking to us on the road, while He was explaining the Scriptures to us?'" (Luke 24:32). The Holy Spirit is our teacher today as we read the Word of God, just as Jesus was Cleopas's teacher, and it is a common experience for believers to sense a burning intensity within as the Holy Spirit brings insight to Scripture.

Scripture itself is a teacher. It enlightens our minds and illuminates the roadway we follow. The psalmist declared: "From Thy precepts I get understanding; therefore I hate every false way. Thy word is a lamp to my feet, and a light to my path" (Ps. 119:104-105). God has a special blessing for those who learn from His law: "Blessed is the man whom Thou dost chasten, O Lord, and dost teach out of Thy law" (Ps. 94:12). Many times I have started the day with a heavy burden, only to find such joy in discoveries in the Bible that my prayers became surprisingly buoyant.

Scripture clarifies the intention of God, if interpreted in faith. The Sadducees did not believe in resurrection and, attempting to trick Jesus, posed an absurd and complicated story about a woman being married seven times to different brothers. Their question about whose wife she would be in the resurrection confused the spiritual nature of the resurrection life. Jesus told them, "'You are mistaken, not understanding the Scriptures, or the power of God'" (Matt. 22:29). We can understand the Scriptures only if we understand the power of God.

The Scriptures will point to Christ as the center of our

124

faith. The Old Testament was a preparation for the work of Christ. When the Jews were angered because Jesus called God His Father (John 5:18), He made several sweeping claims about the nature of His relationship to the Father and concluded these with references to several witnesses about Himself—the witness of John the Baptist, the witness of His own works, the witness of the Father, and the witness of Scripture. He told them, "'You search the Scriptures, because you think that in them you have eternal life; and it is these that bear witness of Me'" (John 5:39). Later the apostle John was to say of his own gospel, "These have been written that you may believe that Jesus is the Christ, the Son of God; and that believing you may have life in His name" (John 20:31).

The ancient practice of meditating on Scripture should form an important part of our devotional life. The Lord told Joshua:

This book of the law shall not depart from your mouth, but you shall meditate on it day and night, so that you may be careful to do according to all that is written in it; for then you will make your way prosperous, and then you will have success (Josh. 1:8).

We enjoy what we are familiar with; and we choose what it is we will be familiar with. Jeremiah, so often very picturesque with his language, said, "Thy words were found and I ate them, and Thy words became for me a joy and the delight of my heart; for I have been called by Thy name, O Lord God of hosts" (Jer. 15:16). Scripture helped shape Jeremiah's prayers, and it should shape ours.

A Time and a Place
The whole concept of the tabernacle and the temple and

stated feasts of the year supports the idea of establishing a regular time and place for our devotions, although, of course, being governed by a new and better testament, we are never slaves to the idea that God is limited by any building, creed, or institution. It is, however, a fact that the greatest men and women of spiritual history have preferred the early morning for their regular devotional exercises. The psalmist said, "In the morning, O Lord, Thou wilt hear my voice; in the morning I will order my prayer to Thee and eagerly watch" (Ps. 5:3).

In my home, the middle bedroom has become the prayer room. Several years ago one of my classes at Southwestern Seminary gave me a kneeling altar, and I have found it to be very helpful. I have several friends who also own kneeling altars, and they also say they have been helpful. Since my wife agrees with me so strongly on the importance of prayer, we are having a kneeling altar made for our granddaughter's room as a gift for her profession of faith. We plan to do the same for our other grandchildren. Later, they will be able to use the altar in their weddings (if they marry), and it will become in their adult life a reminder of the importance of prayer in their lives.

A prayer list may be helpful in covering all the areas for which we need to pray. The writer of Ecclesiastes advised, "Do not be hasty in word or impulsive in thought to bring up a matter in the presence of God" (Eccl. 5:2). Organizing our thoughts in prayer is one means of demonstrating and maintaining reverence. Hosea even suggested taking our repentance to God with the clarity of thought-out words: "Take words with you and return to the Lord. Say to Him, 'Take away all iniquity, and receive us graciously, that we may present the fruit of our lips'" (Hos. 14:2).

A notebook for prayer needs and guidance is useful. I maintain a daily list, a group of people for whom I pray every day. These include all the members of my family, my pastor and staff, my daughter's pastor, several close friends, those in authority over me, and several other continuing concerns. In addition to this, I keep a daily list of temporary concerns which change from time to time, such as the writing of this book, sick friends, or the students in my classes. Then after that, I turn to a weekly list; each day of the week I have a separate list of friends, concerns, convention agencies, agency officials, convention officers, missionaries, governments, and government officials for which I pray. Then I have a monthly list, so that each day of the month I will get around to other items of importance, but somewhat remote from my immediate situation.

For many of these, I write out appropriate Scriptures. For example, I have certain Scriptures that apply to a Christian wife which I often quote to the Lord as I pray for my wife (Prov. 31:10-31; Eph. 5:22-24) or certain Scriptures on the biblical qualifications of a pastor which I use to guide me in praying for my pastor (1 Tim. 3:1-7; 2 Tim. 4:1-2; Titus 1:5-9). In addition, it has been helpful to maintain a list of divine statements and promises that may be used in various prayer situations (Jer. 32:27; 2 Chron. 7:14; 16:9; Isa. 43:1-2).

Very encouraging to my faith has been a list of answered prayers. I neither write down every prayer nor every answer, but certain prayers and answers have proved to be so instructive that I record them so that the lesson will not be lost. This list goes back to 1943!

I do not follow the lists slavishly, but I do find them to be good general guides to prevent prayer from slipping into a selfish orientation, to aid the memory (the mind should pray as well as the spirit), and to assign an order of importance to those things for which we should pray. But there are delightful free periods in my own quiet time when I joyfully follow the Holy Spirit in many matters—concerns, praise, and thanksgiving. For me at least, maintaining a prayer list represents a desire not to appear before God empty-handed (Ex. 34:20).

During my wife's chemotherapy, we gathered so many new insights that we felt we should record as we went along the understandings and the Scriptures which were comforting and instructive. We spent many hours together and separately exploring the profound insights which grew out of Paul's sufferings, especially those recorded in 2 Corinthians. It filled a notebook. We are still digesting it!

Posture may make a difference in attitude. Paul bowed his knees, indicating humility (Eph. 3:14). The elders in the great heavenly scene in Revelation fell on their faces in prostrate adoration (Rev. 11:16). Almost any reverent posture is appropriate, but it is helpful when the body participates in the offering of prayer to a holy God. Of course, it is appropriate to pray anytime and anyplace.

Prayer Anytime and Anywhere

An attitude of prayer at any time or any place should be cultivated. We are to "pray without ceasing" (1 Thess. 5:17); the only activity we carry on ceaselessly is the activity of breathing. In prayer we "breathe" spiritually; this command shows how essential prayer is in the spiritual life. It means that there is no place so unholy that we cannot pray in it. It means that there is no time in which we can afford to ignore God.

It is discourteous to ignore someone who is with you, and Jesus Himself assured us of His continuing presence (Matt. 28:20). He later said to Paul in Corinth, "'Do not be afraid any longer, but go on speaking and do not be silent; for I am with you'" (Acts 18:9-10). Can you imagine Paul ignoring that gracious courtesy? When we ignore Christ, we insult Him.

Admittedly, it is difficult to remember to pray during most of our hectic days. As we are learning, it would be helpful to set aside brief periods for prayer at intervals through the day, as a reminder. If we ask God to remind us, He will do so. Certainly a brief prayer at bedtime is necessary. I also try to use my environment to remind me. For example, sometimes I dress in colors that are suggestive to me of divine attributes—white of purity, green of life, red of sacrifice, and purple of royalty. Then as I go through the day, the very colors I am wearing remind me of the presence of God in my life.

Prayer may be aloud (Rev. 5:12) or silent (1 Sam. 1:13). It may be in a home (Acts 10:9) or on a beach (Acts 21:5). It may be at midnight (Acts 16:25) or in the morning (Ps. 5:3). It may be for a child (Hannah), for life (Hezekiah), or for boldness (the church after Pentecost). Prayer may be made anywhere, anytime, for any holy purpose—and ought to be.

Willingness

A willingness to accept and do God's will should undergird prayer. Jesus' own " 'Not as I will, but as Thou wilt' " is the eternal standard for any relationship with God. It is not the formula " 'Thy will be done' " that secures the divine action, but rather the relationship that grows out of that attitude which enables us to pray within God's will and which places us within the framework where His power is active.

Willingness automatically rules out rebellion, anger, and bitterness if our prayers are not answered as we would like for them to be. Such attitudes are not conducive to a proper relationship and indicate hostility toward God. If we pray for something which God, in His wisdom, knows He cannot give, we may be assured that our ultimate happiness is as important to Him as it is to us. Temporary disappointment may mean eternal gladness.

Willingness is saying to God: "I think I know what is best, but I *know* that You know what is best. I prefer Your judgment to mine." It is acknowledging that God is wiser than we are. It is agreeing that His purposes are grander than ours. It is admitting that our small part of the picture does not include larger designs over a wide canvas that we cannot see.

Willingness does not preclude disappointment and hurt. In the loss of someone we love very much, God is not so unreasonable that He is angry if we mourn or if we express our sense of loss. He is sympathetic when we hurt. Isaiah wrote of God's mercies on Israel, "In all their affliction He was afflicted" (Isa. 63:9). He heard the groaning of the children of Israel (Ex. 2:24). "The Lord is gracious and merciful; slow to anger and great in lovingkindness" (Ps. 145:8).

Willingness rather means that we always participate in God's greater purposes, as Christ did in His Gethsemane prayer. It means that the purposes of our lives are not temporal but eternal. It means that when we hurt, rather than turning from God, we turn to Him and allow Him to comfort us and to help us grow through duress, stress, and loss. Our hurt provides God with an opportunity to give Himself more fully to us. Our willingness means that we are becoming more like Him.

Listening to God

In all the recorded conversations of Noah with God, Noah is pictured as listening. "Noah walked with God" (Gen. 6:9), and yet it was God who did the talking. Repeatedly, the record states: "Then God said to Noah" (Gen. 6:13; see also 7:1; 9:17); "then God spoke to Noah" (Gen. 8:15; 9:8); "and God . . . said to them [Noah and his sons]" (Gen. 9:1). Noah always *responded* to the Lord with obedience: "Thus Noah did; according to all that God had commanded him, so he did" (Gen. 6:22); "Noah did according to all that the Lord had commanded him" (Gen. 7:5); after God said to go out of the ark, "Noah went out" (Gen. 8:18). Can there be any wonder that "God remembered Noah" (Gen. 8:1) or that "God blessed Noah and his sons" (Gen. 9:1)? Noah walked with God by listening to Him and obeying Him.

How do we listen to God? The clearest, least dangerous way is by knowing His Word. God will not work in patterns foreign to the patterns revealed in the Bible. To know the mind of Christ today, it is helpful to be familiar with how He expressed it in His incarnation. We must know His steps and learn to recognize His *kind* of steps.

Troubled by the depth of Judah's sin and yet also by the Lord's use of the Chaldeans (the Babylonians) to punish Judah, Habakkuk asked God to explain this strange use of wickedness to punish God's people, even in their un-righteousness: He said, "I will stand on my guard post and station myself on the rampart; and I will keep watch to see what He will speak to me" (Hab. 2:1). Habakkuk wanted to hear from God and was willing to watch for the answer. Watchfulness, alertness is a part of hearing God; God answered Habakkuk (Hab. 2:2). We must be willing, sensitive, and alert. Long ago another man of God said, "I will hear what God the Lord will say; for He will speak peace to His people, to His godly ones" (Ps. 85:8).

It has also been helpful to me to keep a record of important requests of God and to document the way He works as I pray. That documentation has been very instructive. God works with me as He has worked with me in the past. I have also compared the kind of the things He does for me and in me with the kind of things He did in the biblical record. There is an amazing correspondence. It validates His unchanging nature and provides me with security in knowing what to expect.

I find also that in discerning the leadership of the Lord, I can trust impressions born in submissive prayer and Bible study oriented to the lordship of Christ. I have learned to be suspicious when impressions are born in moments of urgency, irritation, anger, unresolved guilt, or sin of any kind. God works with spirits sensitive to His.

Disobedience of the known will of God is courting disaster. One of the saddest moments in the historical record occurred during the reign of Hoshea, the last king of Israel:

> *Then the king of Assyria carried Israel away into exile to Assyria . . . because they did not obey the voice of the Lord their God, but transgressed His covenant, even all that Moses the servant of the Lord commanded; they would neither listen, nor do it (2 Kings 18:11-12).*

This refusal to hear came at the end of a long record of disobedience. The commands of the Bible are given for obedience, which garners protection and blessing. Disobedience is a strange alternative for a Christian.

The Bible says that "Noah was a righteous man, blameless in his time; Noah walked with God" (Gen. 6:9). The actions we have recorded of his life are those obedient to the various directions he was receiving from God, the building of an altar so that he could sacrifice to the Lord when he was delivered and his dealing with the shameful behavior of his youngest son, Ham. The final action recorded of Noah is a prayer that God would deal with his sons according to their character, a prayer which includes the words "Blessed be the Lord" (Gen. 9:26). History pivoted on one who knew how to listen to God.

Expectancy in Prayer

Hope is one of the most misunderstood words in the New Testament. It means that we start enjoying now what we know is coming by faith; hope is the present pleasure in a future blessing. Hope is expectant; it presents a bright face to God.

Expectancy in prayer should be based on the truth and promises of the Word of God. The ultimate validity of prayer does not depend on human faith but on the Word of God. He honors His own Word. He magnifies His Word in accordance with His own name, all that it identifies, all that it specifies (Ps. 138:8). The most secure thing in the world is truth.

Truth enables waiting. We can wait only if expectancy characterizes our walk and our prayers. Psalm 25:5 provides that note of expectancy: "Lead me in Thy truth and teach me, for Thou art the God of my salvation; for Thee I wait all the day." Paul had a radiant expectancy:

> *I know that this shall turn out for my deliverance [from prison] through your prayers and the provision of the Spirit of Jesus Christ, according to my earnest expectation and hope, that I shall not be put to shame in anything, but that with all boldness, Christ shall even now, as always, be exalted in my body, whether by life or by death (Phil. 1:19-20).*

Waiting can be excruciating if our hope is of the world or worldly. Waiting on God is restful, if we fully understand whom it is we are waiting on. Again, the psalmist said, "My soul, wait in silence for God only, for my hope is from Him" (Ps. 62:5). There is no anxiety in *that* expectant hope; all is quietness and rest. Expectancy does not fidget, and yet it does enjoy the energy that comes from faith.

The Importance of Prayer for Others
The selfish expressions of the disciples stand in stark contrast with the concern of Jesus for others. They quarreled about which of them was regarded as greatest

(Luke 9:46; 22:24); James and John wanted to sit on His right hand (Matt. 20:20-28). Not one selfish thought or action is recorded of Jesus. He owned little and never expressed a desire for anything other than His Father's will.

His prayer for Himself occupies five verses of the twenty-six verses in the high-priestly prayer of John 17 so that a certain kind of thought for self is permissible. Yet even in these five verses He is praying for the restoration of a right order which will make salvation available for all people (vv. 2-3). In other words, His prayer for Himself carries within it benevolence for others. Twenty-one other verses are given to prayer for His disciples and those who would come afterwards. Paul commented, "Even Christ did not please Himself" (Rom. 15:3). The noblest of the descriptions of Christ's unselfishness is that of 2 Corinthians 8:9: "You know the grace of our Lord Jesus Christ, that though He was rich, yet for your sake He became poor, that you through His poverty might become rich."

This ideal became the standard for the believers in the New Testament church. Jesus had redefined who our neighbor is (Luke 10:30-37). He had placed the command to love one's neighbor second to the command to love God (Mark 12:28-31). The continuing unfolding of new revelation would be consistent with the life and teaching of Jesus. Paul enjoined the Corinthians, "Let no one seek his own good, but that of his neighbor" (1 Cor. 10:24).

Our prayer must match our life, and our life should match our prayer. Repeatedly Paul poured out his heart in his prayers for the churches, and his travels and work with them match his prayers. He refused to accept money from the Corinthian church (1 Cor. 9:1-15; 2 Cor. 11:7-9), but he taught them, preached to them, and prayed for them. He told them, "I also please all men in all things, not seeking my own profit, but the profit of the many, that they may be saved" (1 Cor. 10:33). We always pray in the character of

God. That character is seen perfectly in the person of Christ; it is reflected in Paul and is to be reflected in all disciples who seek the glory of God and the coming of His kingdom.

Family and Group Prayer

As I was pastoring a church on an interim basis in the spring of 1985, I tried to develop a spirit of prayer in that body by example and teaching. In the first Wednesday evening service, I asked every member present (there were sixty-seven) to fill out a card giving his or her greatest prayer needs; the card would be for private use by me alone. I then took those cards and prayed daily for each person according to the needs mentioned. We began to see an unusual work of the Lord.

In spite of a prayerful spirit that grew in the body and a beautiful self-giving that many in the church were exhibiting, I discovered early that only a few of the families were practicing family devotions. After that, in ministering to many churches and seminary students, I began to uncover the fact that the "family altar" (as my family always called it) is exceedingly rare among Christians—even among ministers and leaders.

The usual excuse people make is that they cannot find a time when all the family will remain still together for a few minutes. Time, of course, is a major problem in the hectic diversity of activities—church, business, sports, television, educational activities—that most families feel obligated to maintain. There can be no question that time is a serious, difficult, major problem.

But the lack of mutual prayer together is a more serious, difficult, and weighty problem. Families will not establish the practice of family devotions until they become convinced that it is more important than their other activities. The problem of prayerless families is probably only a symptom of the larger problem of prayerless people.

Perhaps what we need are models. If, in the churches where this book is taught, godly men and women would determine that *their* families could become models for other families, we might see a movement developing. I would like to suggest that the pastor and his wife in every church firmly commit their home to family prayer and that they enlist other spiritual leaders in the church to do the same.

Several people have confessed to me that they do not have family devotions because they are self-conscious about it. Often the father has said that he feels he is supposed to be a teacher in that situation but that his wife knows so much more about the Bible than he that he is embarrassed. Both the husband and wife must be supportive of prayer in the home. Neither should assume a superior or a demanding attitude. Each should help the other as they provide spiritual leadership for the family.

Our family altar is a time of mutual sharing. After we read a Bible passage together, we each share and discuss prayerfully opinions and ideas about what we have read, about our life together, about the church, about events in the work of the Lord that our prayers might touch, or about family and friends who need prayer. We do not feel obligated to pose wise solutions or to appear spiritual. We simply talk. For us, it is never formal or fussy, self-conscious or posed, just friendly, with the interest vested in the glory of God and the progress of His work. And then each of us prays. Sometimes one of us prays a long prayer or an unusually heartfelt prayer, but there is never an ensuing obligation to "match the quality" of anybody else's prayer. In other words, there is a great freedom simply to be ourselves. The family altar is no time to prove anything.

We have found the early morning to be ideal. I usually rise in the early hours of the morning (which means I must go to bed early—and I do). My wife also gets up early. Often we will eat a simple breakfast to allow more time for our devotions together. Then after breakfast we enjoy our time together with the Lord.

It gives me a security about my work day that is irreplaceable. By the time I go to work, I have realized anew that God is still on His Throne. I also have experienced a sense of His love for me and His provision for my day's needs. I have secured the endorsement of my wife's prayers, and I know that she will continue to pray with me and for me as I face the day.

If a family cannot manage an early-morning time, with children to get to school, then sometime during the evening they might work it in. The sacrifice of one television program is not much to give up for the eternal value of time with the Lord. Ideally, if it is in the evening, the best time would be just before bedtime. I grew up with such a family time, and it contributed greatly to my sense of security.

The church also must pray together, with mutuality of spirit. It is true that prayer rooms and prayer chains contribute greatly to the life of a church, but there is no substitute for praying together. Mutual prayer distributes the burdens of the church so that all can carry the work of prayer home for the rest of the week.

Prayer binds the church together as nothing else can. Most congregations sing together but do very little else together. We are often involved in small-group projects, but the whole church does little together. The greater part of the usual public service, Sunday or midweek, is spent listening passively, to a preacher, to a soloist, or to a choir. We worship with the soloist or choir, we receive spiritual insight from the preacher, but it is equally important for the church to agree in prayer.

The privilege of mutual assent, whether with one leader or with a group of alternating leaders in prayer, is a high and noble advantage that only Christians have. It is the proof that God is indeed the Father of all of us who have received

Christ, and that we are, after all, the family of God.

PERSONAL LEARNING ACTIVITY 14
Do you need to improve your prayer and devotional life?
Rate yourself by circling the proper response.
1. I have a regular time for prayer.   Yes   No
2. I read the Bible daily as part of my   Yes   No
   devotional activity.
3. I pray for others, as well as for my own   Yes   No
   needs.
4. I maintain an active prayer list and use it   Yes   No
   daily.
5. I can name specific answers to prayer in my   Yes   No
   life in the past three months.

Epilogue

Trying to cover all the aspects of prayer is somewhat like trying to explain infinity. Prayer, like its author, is inexhaustible. The prayer life of every Christian will bear a unique mold because the prayer calling of every Christian is unique. God relates to every individual on that person's unique and private terms. In my study of the prayers of the Bible, I discovered that each of the great prayer warriors of the Bible had patterns peculiar to himself or herself. Every Christian should determine through prayer what is that one pattern and purpose of prayer which God wants to use in his or her life.

The prayer life will bring tests. I get calls every week about aspects of prayer from people who are interested but confused, from some who are disappointed, from some who are very sincere but who have not gone as far with God as they thought they had. The road is ever upward and is narrow. Tests are one of the ways God has of rerouting us when we get off the narrow road.

Many of our prayers are in an ignorance which we cannot help. A dear friend of mine prayed last summer that her baby would live. It did not. We simply do not always know what is best, and we can only pray as best we know how. Abraham's prayer in ignorance (Gen. 18:23-32) remains a beautiful proof that it is all right to pray in ignorance, outside the specific will of God, if we are praying within the character of God.

One of the problems we face perpetually is the human dilemma of moving rather awkwardly toward the throne we are to rule from. Full dominion has not yet been restored (Rom. 8:18-25), and the waiting while we learn is part of our training. Endurance is the temporal expression of immutability, and we are to become like

God, not in attribute, but in all aspects of character.

That is the basic purpose of prayer. You become like what you spend time with. You know best what you spend time with. In fellowship with God we are learning His character and expressing His character to the world. That is why He honors prayer—so that His character will indeed be expressed to the world. That is why prayer is, after all, the most powerful force available to Christians. We are part of a plan grander than the greatest minds can conceive, holier than any prophet can describe, richer than human language can explore. The grandest, holiest, most dynamic events in the cosmos are being brought about through prayer. And it is being done by seemingly normal, average, ordinary people who someday will sit on thrones of unimaginable authority and dominion.

For Further Study

Edwards, Judy. *How to Pray for Missions*. Birmingham: Woman's Missionary Union. Available April 1987.

Hunt, T. W., and Catherine Walker. *PrayerLife: Walking in Fellowship with God*. Nashville: The Sunday School Board of the Southern Baptist Convention. Available January 1988.

Teaching Guide

Arthur H. Criscoe

Introduction

This teaching guide contains detailed teaching plans to assist you in leading a group study of *The Doctrine of Prayer*. The plans can be used with either a large or small group.

In addition to *The Doctrine of Prayer,* you will need a copy of *The Doctrine of Prayer—Teaching Workbook*. The teaching workbook contains a supply of overhead cel masters, worksheet masters, teaching posters, and discussion cards. These resources provide visual aids to enrich the sessions and other tools to involve group members actively in the learning process. Group size is no problem; the resources are effective with large auditorium groups and with small groups in a classroom.

One copy of the teaching workbook is needed. The cel masters, worksheet masters, posters, and discussion cards may be reproduced. Suggestions for using all of the resources can be found in this teaching guide as well as in the teaching workbook itself.

Learning Goals
Upon completion of this course, each group member should have a better understanding of the doctrine of prayer and its implications for his or her life and also should become personally involved in developing an effective prayer life.

Each session has specific, measurable learning goals related to these overall goals. The learning goals will help you to maintain a focus as you lead each session. They also afford a means by which participants can measure their progress along the way.

Advance Planning
Before you make specific plans to lead the sessions, complete the following actions.
1. Work with the proper persons to publicize the study through pulpit announcements, church bulletin or newsletter, and bulletin boards. See that announcements are made in each Adult Sunday School class and Church Training group.
2. Order an adequate supply of *The Doctrine of Prayer* well in advance of the study. Enlist participants prior to the study and get copies of *The Doctrine of Prayer* to them. Assign chapter 1 for study before the first session.
3. Prepare a poster outline of the session titles. This poster will be used in all of the sessions. Prepare a 1 by 4 arrow pointer from poster board and glue the arrow to a clothespin. Use this pointer with the outline poster.

Session 1:	The Foundation of Prayer—the God Who Cares (Chapter 1)
Session 2:	Jesus—the Example of Prayer The Holy Spirit—Our Helper in Prayer (Chapters 2 and 3)
Session 3:	The Ways People Pray Questions about Prayer (Chapters 4 and 5)
Session 4:	Hindrances to Effective Prayer Prayer in the Church—Then and Now (Chapters 6 and 7)
Session 5:	Developing an Effective Prayer Life (Chapter 8)

4. As a part of your advance preparation, study the entire text and complete the personal learning activities well ahead of time. Read the teaching guide for each session. This study will acquaint you with the doctrine and will alert you to any long-range plans you need to make.
5. Prepare the resources found in the teaching workbook.
   • Prepare a set of overhead cels from the masters in the teaching workbook. Posters and sentence strips (using adding-machine tape) can be made from the masters if you do not have an overhead projector.
   • Prepare a set of the teaching posters. Use poster board or newsprint and felt-tip markers of different colors. Enlist other persons to assist you in preparing the posters.
   • Prepare packets of discussion cards. Duplicate enough cards to have a set for every four or five persons in your group.
6. Obtain and listen to the two Broadman cassette tapes "The Doctrine of Prayer, Volume 1 and 2" by William H. Stephens. These tapes are for you, the leader. They are designed to give you background and supplementary information and to lead you through the eight chapters of *The Doctrine of Prayer*. These tapes will help you to teach from an overflow of knowledge.
7. Obtain a roll of newsprint or white paper, a roll of adding-machine tape (for making sentence and word strips), pencils, felt-tip pens, chalkboard, chalk, eraser, and masking tape.
8. Review the Church Study Course information in the back of the book. You may want to enlist a person in advance to be responsible for registering participants and for keeping a record of attendance.

Planning for Each Session
After you have done advance planning, plan each session.

1. Read and study the appropriate chapters in *The Doctrine of Prayer*. Carefully study the suggested teaching guide for the session. Work through the learning activities in advance and decide which ones to use. Plan how you will adapt the session to fit the needs and interests of the members.
2. Prepare your own teaching plan. Plan how much time you will allow for each activity. You will want to be flexible and sensitive to the needs of members and not be rushed in moving through the session. At the same time, you will want to have a tentative time schedule in mind for the session.
3. Prepare any learning aids that you will need for the session. Obtain other materials you will need.
4. Make any assignments to individuals well in advance. Be sure the person understands the assignment and knows where to find help in preparing it.
5. Arrange the meeting room properly before each session begins. The room arrangement should create an atmosphere conducive to learning.
6. Use your imagination in preparing for and leading the sessions. Do not feel bound by the suggestions in this guide.
7. Pray for the guidance of the Holy Spirit as you prepare for and lead the sessions.

SESSION 1

The Foundation of Prayer— the God Who Cares

Chapter 1

Learning goal: After completing this session, participants should have a better understanding of prayer and of how prayer is related to the nature of God. Participants will be able to: (1) explain in what ways prayer is universal and (2) identify two attributes of God related specifically to prayer.

Before the Session

1. Have copies of *The Doctrine of Prayer* available for participants. Have registration materials and a Baptist Doctrine Diploma available.

2. Duplicate worksheets 1, 2, and 3 from *The Doctrine of Prayer—Teaching Workbook.*

3. Prepare overhead cels or posters of cel masters 1, 2, 3, 4, and 5 from the teaching workbook.

4. Prepare the teaching posters for chapter 1 from the teaching workbook. Mount the posters in random order.

5. Prepare the discussion cards for chapter 1 from the teaching workbook.

6. Prepare a brief lecture or summary of the topic "Prayer Is Universal."

7. Prepare four 3 by 5 cards with the following Scripture references:

- Psalm 18:2; 23; 46:1; John 10:7.
- Psalm 17:8; 31:3; Deuteronomy 33:27; John 10:11.
- Psalm 36:7; 84:11; 94:22; John 15:5.
- Psalm 91:4; Deuteronomy 32:9-11; Mark 2:19; Hebrews 2:11.

Along with the Scripture references on each card, write these two questions: (1) What terms or illustrations are used in these passages to teach that God is near to help us? (2) What is the main teaching of the passages?

8. Prepare a brief lecture or summary of the topics "Prayer Is Based on the Nature of God" and "Prayer Is Effective Because God Has Chosen to Hear When We Call to Him."

During the Session

1. Greet members as they arrive. Have the overhead cel or poster of cel 1 projected or displayed as a center of attention. Distribute copies of worksheet 2 and ask members to complete them before the session begins.

2. Make any needed introductions and help everyone to feel at ease. Quickly care for record keeping and administrative matters. Distribute copies of *The Doctrine of Prayer*. Show the Baptist Doctrine Diploma and encourage everyone to earn one.

3. Ask members to find the first mention of prayer in the Bible and the last recorded prayer in the Bible. (Gen. 4:26; Rev. 22:20). Allow two minutes for this and lead a brief discussion. Emphasize the importance of prayer in the Bible and in our lives today. Explain that the word *doctrine* means *teaching* so that doctrine of prayer is a study of what the Bible teaches concerning prayer.

4. Use cel 2 to overview the entire study. Use cel 3 to share the overall goals for the entire study. Focus on session 1 and tell the learning goal for this session. Lead in prayer.

5. Distribute copies of worksheet 3. Ask volunteers to read the statements aloud. As each statement is read, determine those who agree with the statement, those who disagree with the statement, and those who are undecided. If the group is divided in opinion, allow time for discussion of the statement.

6. Write three headings across the chalkboard: *Scripture,*

Prayer Request, and *Answer.* Beneath *Scripture* list 1 Samuel 1:9-11,19-20; 2 Kings 20:1-6; Acts 9:36-41; Acts 12:1-9. Divide members into four small groups and assign each group one of the Scripture passages. Allow time for small-group work and call for reports. Complete the chart as reports are given.

7. Lecture briefly on the topic "Prayer Is Universal." Use cel 4 as a visual aid. (Leave the two remaining points covered until later in the session.) Refer to worksheet 2 to illustrate the universality of prayer.

8. Lecture briefly on the topic "Prayer Is Based on the Nature of God" and "Prayer Is Effective Because God Has Chosen to Hear When We Call to Him." Use cel 4 as a visual aid.

9. Use the same four groups and distribute the cards prepared in point 7 in "Before the Session." Allow time for group work and call for reports.

10. Show cel 5. Ask for volunteers to identify Corrie ten Boom. (She lived 1892-1983. A native of Holland, she and her sister Betsie were placed in a concentration camp at Ravensbruck during World War II because their father sheltered Jews in a secret room in their house. Following World War II Corrie traveled all over the world telling people of God's love and care.) Refer to personal learning activity (PLA) 1 and allow time for members to share their responses.

11. Distribute the discussion cards. Ask volunteers to read the cards and share their responses.

12. Call attention to the teaching posters on the walls. Ask for volunteers to read the statements and to comment on their meanings.

13. Distribute copies of worksheet 1, "Pretest/Posttest," and ask members to complete the pretest before the next session.

14. Close with prayer.

SESSION 2

Jesus—the Example of Prayer
The Holy Spirit—Our Helper in Prayer

Chapters 2 and 3

Learning goal: After completing this session, participants should have a better understanding of Jesus' practice and teaching on prayer and of the work of the Holy Spirit in relation to prayer. Participants will be able to: (1) describe in their own words the prayer life of Jesus; (2) summarize in their own words what Jesus taught concerning prayer; and (3) describe the work of the Holy Spirit in relation to prayer.

Before the Session

1. Duplicate worksheets 4, 5, and 6 from the teaching workbook.
2. Prepare cels or posters of cel masters 6, 7, 8, 9, and 10 from the teaching workbook.
3. Prepare the teaching posters for chapters 2 and 3 from the teaching workbook. Mount the posters in random order on the walls.
4. Prepare the discussion cards for chapters 2 and 3 from the teaching workbook.
5. Prepare a brief lecture on chapter 3.

During the Session

1. Distribute copies of worksheet 4 as members arrive. Instruct them to complete the worksheet as a presession activity. Take up worksheet 1 and save for session 5.

2. Welcome members. Use cel 2 to overview this session. Share the overall learning goal for this session.

3. Show cel 6. Mention that this prayer is associated with Francis of Assisi. Francis spent his life ministering to the needy and died at the age of forty-five. Lead members in reading this prayer in unison. Then read the remainder of the prayer not shown on the cel.

O Divine Master, grant that I may not so much seek
to be consoled as to console,
to be understood as to understand,
to be loved as to love;
for it is in giving that we receive,
it is in pardoning that we are pardoned, and
it is in dying that we are born to eternal life.

---

4. Explain that conversational prayer is a group talking together with God. Only one subject at a time is prayed about, and each person prays only one or two sentences at a time. "Amen" is not used at the end of each short prayer, since it is all one prayer. Take the petition "Let me sow love" from Francis's prayer and lead in a time of conversational prayer on this subject.

5. Spend a few minutes discussing worksheet 4.

6. Distribute copies of worksheet 5 and ask members to work with a partner in completing them. After a few minutes of work lead in a discussion of the prayer life of Jesus.

7. Refer to PLA 3 and ask volunteers to call out answers.

8. Use cel 7 as a visual aid to move into a discussion of what Jesus taught concerning prayer. Distribute copies of worksheet 6 and ask members to work with the partner again in completing them. Call for responses and lead in a discussion of the high-priestly prayer of John 17.

9. Lead in a discussion of the Model Prayer in Matthew 6, using cel 8 as a teaching aid.

10. Briefly summarize chapter 3, using cel 9 as a teaching aid. Ask members to respond to PLA 6.

11. Use the discussion cards to involve members in reflecting on the key points of the session.

12. Refer to the teaching posters. Ask members to select a sign, read it to the group, and comment on its meaning.

13. Show cel 10. Read Hebrews 13:20-21 as a benediction.

SESSION 3

The Ways People Pray Questions About Prayer

Chapters 4 and 5

Learning goal: After completing this session, participants should have a better understanding of the different types of prayer and of some of the common questions asked about prayer. Participants will be able to: (1) name five types or forms of prayer; (2) recognize each type or form; and (3) answer questions about prayer.

Before the Session

1. Duplicate worksheets 7, 8, and 9 from the teaching workbook.

2. Prepare cels or posters of cel masters 11, 12, 13, and 14 from the teaching workbook.

3. Prepare the teaching posters for chapters 4 and 5 from the teaching workbook. Mount the posters in random order on the walls.

4. Prepare the discussion cards for chapters 4 and 5 from the teaching workbook.

5. Read 1 Kings 17—18 to prepare to lead a discussion of Elijah's prayer in 1 Kings 18:36-37.

6. Prepare four 3 by 5 cards with the following Scripture references:

- Acts 4:23-31; Psalm 43:1; 51:1-14; 103:1-5; 104:1; John 17:15-21.
- Psalm 54:1-3; 111; 1 Peter 1:3-4; Acts 12:5; 1 Samuel

1:9-11; Luke 5:8.
- Psalm 56:1-4; Luke 18:13; Matthew 8:1-2; Exodus 32:31-32; Ephesians 1:3; Job 42:1-6.
- Psalm 59:1-5; 147; Luke 23:34; John 4:46-50; Ephesians 1:15-20.

Include these instructions on each card: Read each Scripture reference and determine the type or form of prayer made (adoration, intercession, petition, repentance, deliverance).

During the Session

1. Welcome members. Show cel 11. Point out the simplicity, yet intellectual depth of the fisherman's prayer. Give an opportunity for members to share prayer requests. Use the fisherman's prayer as a part of your opening prayer.
2. Use cel 2 to review briefly and to overview this session. Share the overall learning goal for this session.
3. Distribute copies of worksheet 7 and spend a few minutes discussing the statements.
4. Use cel 12 to lead in a discussion of chapter 4. Reveal the points one at a time and ask members to define or describe each type or form of prayer as it is revealed.
5. Show cel 13 and involve members in analyzing Elijah's prayer on Mount Carmel. Be sure the following characteristics are mentioned: brief, serious, simple language, and grounded in the covenant-keeping nature of God.
6. Divide members into four small groups. Give each group one of the cards that you prepared with Scripture references on prayers. Ask each group to study the prayers referred to and to determine the type or form of each prayer. Allow a few minutes for small-group work and call for reports.
7. Distribute small slips of paper. Ask members to write down any questions they have about prayer. Collect the slips for use later in the session.

8. Show cel 14 and lead a brief discussion of each question. Be sensitive not to give quick, pat answers yourself but lead members to formulate their own answers, using chapter 5 as a resource.

9. Distribute copies of worksheet 8. Ask members to turn to a partner and take turns responding to the questions.

10. Discuss the questions that members wrote on small slips of paper.

11. Involve members in giving responses to the discussion cards on chapters 4 and 5.

12. Refer to the teaching posters. Ask for volunteers to read the signs and to comment on the meaning of each one.

13. Distribute copies of worksheet 9 and ask members to complete them at home.

14. Close by asking members to write brief prayers of adoration. Ask volunteers to share their prayers.

SESSION 4

Hindrances to Effective Prayer
Prayer in the Church—Then and Now

Chapters 6 and 7

Learning goal: After completing this session, participants should have a better understanding of the primary hindrances to prayer and of the role of prayer in the life of the church. Participants will be able to: (1) name six primary hindrances to prayer; (2) identify the biggest hindrance to prayer in their own lives; (3) resolve to take at least one action to overcome the hindrances to prayer in their lives; (4) summarize the role of prayer in the life of the early church; and (5) summarize the role of prayer in their church today.

Before the Session

1. Duplicate worksheets 10 and 11 from the teaching workbook.
2. Prepare cels or posters of cel masters 15, 16, 17, and 18 from the teaching workbook.
3. Prepare the teaching posters for chapters 6 and 7 from the teaching workbook. Mount the posters in random order on the walls.
4. Prepare the discussion cards for chapters 6 and 7 from

the teaching workbook.

5. Prepare a brief lecture on chapter 7.

During the Session

1. Distribute copies of worksheet 10 to members as they enter the room and ask them to complete them before the session begins.

2. Welcome members. Ask them to call out the names of hymns they can think of about prayer. Lead the group in singing a hymn about prayer.

3. Show cel 15 and give members an opportunity to comment on the prayer of the African girl. Call for prayer requests and ask a volunteer to lead in prayer.

4. Use cel 2 to review briefly and to overview this session. State the overall learning goal for this session.

5. Spend a few minutes discussing worksheet 10.

6. Show cel 16 and lead in a discussion of the six hindrances listed. Lead members to identify other hindrances and write them in the blank blocks on the cel.

7. Ask members to share the biggest hindrance to effective prayer they face personally. Then lead members to share specific actions they can take to overcome the hindrances to prayer in their lives.

8. Lecture briefly on chapter 7. Use cel 17 as a teaching aid.

9. Distribute copies of worksheet 11. Ask members to turn to a partner and work together to complete the worksheet. Allow time for this work and then call for reporting.

10. Ask members to tell about the practice of prayer in their childhood homes.

11. Involve members in giving responses to the discussion cards on chapters 6 and 7.

12. Refer to the teaching posters. Ask for volunteers to read the signs and to comment on the meaning of each one.

13. Show cel 18. Spend a few minutes explaining David's prayer of repentance. Close with prayer.

SESSION 5

Developing an Effective Prayer Life

Chapter 8

Learning Goal: After completing this session, participants should have a better understanding of how to develop an effective prayer life and should be committed personally to developing and strengthening their own prayer lives. Participants will be able to: (1) name at least four key factors in an effective prayer life and (2) outline plans for strengthening their own prayer lives.

Before the Session
1. Duplicate worksheets 12, 13, and 1, "Pretest/Posttest," from the teaching workbook.
2. Prepare cels or posters of cel masters 19 and 20 from the teaching workbook.
3. Prepare the teaching posters for chapter 8 from the teaching workbook. Mount the posters in random order on the walls.
4. Prepare the discussion cards for chapter 8 from the teaching workbook.
5. Prepare a brief lecture on chapter 8.

During the Session
1. Welcome members. Call for prayer requests and ask a volunteer to lead in prayer.

2. Use cel 2 to review briefly and to overview this session. Tell the overall learning goal for this session.

3. Distribute copies of worksheet 12 and spend a few minutes discussing the statements.

4. Lecture briefly on chapter 8. Use cel 19 as a teaching aid.

5. Involve members in sharing responses to the discussion cards on chapter 8.

6. Refer to the teaching posters. Ask for volunteers to read the signs and to comment on the meaning of each one.

7. Refer to PLA 14. Allow time for members to complete the self-evaluation. Challenge members to write two actions they will take to improve in a weak area.

8. Ask each member to work with a partner to outline and to tell plans for strengthening his or her own prayer life. Allow a few minutes for this work and then allow time for reporting. Be sensitive and do not make anyone uncomfortable who might not wish to tell his or her plans.

9. Distribute copies of worksheet 13 and allow a few minutes for completion. Lead in a time of sharing.

10. Distribute copies of worksheet 1 and allow time for members to complete the posttest. Call for volunteers to give their responses by comparing what they wrote with the pretest they took after session 1. Allow time for members to express thoughts about any part of the study.

11. Express appreciation to members for their attendance and participation in the study.

12. Show cel 20. Ask group members to join hands. Pray this prayer as a closure to the study.

After the Session

1. Complete the request form for Church Study Course credit.

2. Be sure to turn in your registration and attendance records to the proper person.

3. Take time to do a thorough evaluation of the entire study.

The Church Study Course

The Church Study Course is a Southern Baptist educational system consisting of short courses for adults and youth. It is complete with recognition, records, and reports. More than five hundred courses are available in twenty-three subject areas. Credit is awarded for each course completed. These credits may be applied to one or more of the 125 plus diploma plans in the recognition system. Diplomas are available for most leadership positions, as well as are general diplomas for all Christians. These diplomas are the certification that a person has completed from five to eight prescribed courses. Diploma requirements are given in the catalog.

Complete details about the Church Study Course system, courses available, and diplomas offered may be found in a current copy of Church Study Course Catalog. Study course materials are available from Baptist Book Stores.

The Church Study Course system is sponsored by the Sunday School Board, the Woman's Missionary Union, and the Brotherhood Commission of the Southern Baptist Convention.

How to Request Credit for This Course

This book is the text for course number 05052 in the subject area Baptist Doctrine. This course is designed for a minimum of five hours of group study.

Requirements for Credit

Credit may be earned in two ways.

1. *Group Study.* Read the book and attend group sessions. (If you are absent from one or more sessions, complete the learning activities for the material missed.)

2. *Individual study.* Read the book and complete the learning activities. (Written work should be submitted to an appropriate church leader.)

To Request Credit

A request for credit may be made on Form 725, Church Study Course Enrollment/Credit Request, and sent to the Awards Office, Sunday School Board, 127 Ninth Avenue, North, Nashville, TN 37234. The form on the following page may be used to request credit.

A record of your awards will be maintained by the Awards Office. Within three months of your completion of a course, a copy of your transcript will be sent to your church for distribution to you.

CHURCH STUDY COURSE
ENROLLMENT/CREDIT REQUEST (FORM-725)

INSTRUCTIONS:

1. Please PRINT or TYPE.
2. COURSE CREDIT REQUEST—Requirements must be met. Use exact title.
3. ENROLLMENT IN DIPLOMA PLANS—Enter selected diploma title to enroll.
4. For additional information see the Church Study Course Catalog.
5. Duplicate additional forms as needed. Free forms are available from the Awards Office and State Conventions.

PERSONAL CSC NUMBER (If Known)

TYPE OF REQUEST: (Check all that apply)

☐ Course Credit
☐ Enrollment in Diploma Plan

☐ Address Change
☐ Name Change
☐ Church Change

☐ Mr.   ☐ Miss
☐ Mrs.

DATE OF BIRTH

Month	Day	Year

REQUEST FOR

Name (First, MI, Last)

Street, Route, or P.O. Box

City, State, Zip Code

CHURCH

Church Name

Mailing Address

City, State, Zip Code

COURSE CREDIT REQUEST

Course No	Use exact title
05052	1. *The Doctrine of Prayer*
Course No	2. Use exact title
Course No	3. Use exact title
Course No	4. Use exact title
Course No	5. Use exact title

ENROLLMENT IN DIPLOMA PLANS

If you have not previously indicated a diploma(s) you wish to earn, or you are beginning work on a new one(s), select and enter the diploma title from the current Church Study Course Catalog. Select one that relates to your leadership responsibility or interest. When all requirements have been met, the diploma will be automatically mailed to your church. No charge will be made for enrollment or diplomas.

Title of diploma	Age group or area
1.	

Title of diploma	Age group or area
2.	

Signature of Pastor, Teacher, or Study Leader	Date

MAIL THIS REQUEST TO

CHURCH STUDY COURSE AWARDS OFFICE
RESEARCH SERVICES DEPARTMENT
127 NINTH AVENUE, NORTH
NASHVILLE, TENNESSEE 37234

23 - 019

FORM-725 (Rev. 7-83)